AGS

PR
GUIDE TO
*B*ETTER
ENGLISH

MW01247756

Level II

Teacher's Guide

AGS®
American Guidance Service, Inc.
Circle Pines, Minnesota 55014-1796
1-800-328-2560

Printed in the United States of America

ISBN 0-7854-1797-4

Product Number 93079

A 0 9 8 7 6 5 4 3 2 1

CONTENTS

AGS Practical Guide to Better English

PROGRAM GOAL

The Practical Guide to Better English program is designed to help high school students and adults gain an awareness of the basic elements of the English language and develop proficiency in all the skills necessary for successful written communication in school and in the workplace.

OBJECTIVES

This new four-level program has the following objectives:

• Develop students' *mastery of essential grammar, usage, and mechanics skills* through focused instruction and practice.

• Build students' *vocabulary and store of background knowledge* through the use of informative, interesting real-world content.

• Improve students' *writing skills at the sentence, paragraph, and whole-composition levels* through the use of accessible models and directed practice in the various writing domains.

• Build students' *self-sufficiency in revising and proofreading* by providing a complete Handbook of grammar, usage, and mechanics rules bound into each pupil book. Students can use this as a resource when they revise written work in other classes and outside school.

Scope and Sequence of Grammar, Usage, and Mechanics Skills

	LEVEL I	II	III	IV
CAPITALIZATION				
Capitalize first word in sentence	•	•	•	•
Capitalize proper nouns	•	•	•	•
Capitalize proper adjectives	•	•	•	•
Capitalize days of week	•	•	•	•
Capitalize months NOT seasons	•	•	•	•
Capitalize holidays, festivals	•	•	•	•
Capitalize the word *I*	•	•	•	•
CAPITALIZATION WITH PUNCTUATION				
Capitalize initial; use period		•	•	•
Capitalize personal title; use period		•	•	•
Capitalize abbreviations of day, week, month; use period		•	•	•
Capitals in addresses, punctuation		•	•	•
Commas in address in sentence		•	•	•
Capitalize words in titles		•	•	•
Draw line under title of book, movie		•	•	•
Quotation marks around title of poem, story		•	•	•
Direct vs. indirect quotations			•	•
Punctuate direct quotations		•	•	•
Commas in direct quotations		•	•	•
End punctuation in direct quotations		•	•	•
Quote inside quote: single quotation marks			•	•
OTHER USES OF COMMAS				
Comma in date (or no)	•	•	•	•
Comma after day, year	•	•	•	•
Comma after name, direct address		•	•	•
Comma after introductory word		•	•	•
Commas to set off interrupting word				•
Comma in compound sentence		•	•	•
Comma after introductory dependent clause			•	•
Commas to set off nonrestrictive clauses				•
Commas in series	•	•	•	•
Comma to separate adjectives				•
Appositive			•	•
Commas to set off appositive			•	•
PARTS OF SPEECH				
Nouns	•	•	•	•
Proper nouns	•	•	•	•
Nouns—singular and plural	•	•	•	•

	LEVEL I	II	III	IV
Plural: most add *-s*	•	•	•	•
Plural with *ch, sh, s, x, z*	•	•	•	•
Plural with *f* or *fe*	•	•	•	•
Plural with consonant + *y*	•	•	•	•
Plural with vowel + *y*	•	•	•	•
Plurals: irregular	•	•	•	•
Some plurals same as singular	•	•	•	•
Possessive nouns	•	•	•	•
Possessive nouns: form singular with *'s*		•	•	•
Possessive nouns: plural ending in *-s* and NOT ending in *-s*			•	•
Pronouns: personal	•	•	•	•
Pronouns: subject		•	•	•
Pronouns: as direct object			•	•
Pronouns: object of preposition			•	•
Pronouns: *I* or *me* last in pair or series			•	•
Pronouns preceding nouns			•	•
Pronouns: compound personal	•			•
Pronouns: interrogative				•
Pronouns: demonstrative				•
Verbs: action, being	•	•	•	•
Verb phrase; helping verbs		•	•	•
Agreement in number	•	•	•	•
Agreement: *you are/were*	•	•	•	•
Agreement: *there is/are*		•	•	•
Agreement: compound subjects with *and/or*				•
Verbs: principal parts		•	•	•
First principal part			•	•
Second principal part			•	•
Third principal part			•	•
Present participle			•	•
Second and third principal parts sometimes the same			•	•
Simple verb tenses: past, present, future			•	•
Perfect tenses			•	•
Contractions	•	•	•	•
Adjectives	•	•	•	•
Articles (*an* before vowel)	•	•	•	•
Adjectives: demonstrative			•	•
Possessives act as adjectives			•	•
Use adjective (not adverb) as predicate adjective			•	•

Scope and Sequence of Grammar, Usage, and Mechanics Skills

	I	II	III	IV
Adjectives: comparative/superlative	•		•	•
Adverbs	•	•	•	•
Adverbs modify verbs	•	•	•	•
Adverbs modify adjectives			•	•
Adverbs modify adverbs			•	•
Don't confuse adverbs and adjectives			•	•
Adverbs: comparative/superlative				•
Prepositions	•	•	•	•
Prepositional phrases/elements		•	•	•
Prepositional phrases: adjectival			•	•
Prepositional phrases: adverbial			•	•
Prepositions: pairs with different meanings		•	•	•
Conjunctions: coordinating		•	•	•
Conjunctions: subordinating		•	•	•
Combining sentences	•	•	•	•
Interjections			•	•
VERBALS				
Verbals				•
Participle/participial phrase				•
Infinitive/infinitive phrase				•
Gerund/gerund phrase				•
TROUBLESOME VERBS				
Teach vs. *learn*	•	•	•	•
May vs. *can*	•	•	•	•
Sit vs. *set*	•	•	•	•
Lie (verb)		•	•	•
Lay (verb)		•	•	•
WORD STUDY				
Synonyms	•	•	•	•
Prepositional phrase used instead of a single word			•	•
Antonyms	•	•	•	•
Unnecessary words, eliminating	•	•	•	•
Negatives	•	•	•	•
Unsuitable expressions, eliminating	•	•	•	•
Homophones	•	•	•	•
SENTENCES				
Sentence/fragment/run-on/comma splice	•	•	•	•
Sentence: declarative	•	•	•	•
Sentence: interrogative	•	•	•	•

	I	II	III	IV
Sentence: imperative			•	•
Sentence: exclamatory	•	•	•	•
Subject/predicate—simple subject	•	•	•	•
Compound subject			•	•
Complete subject			•	•
Simple predicate	•		•	•
Compound predicate			•	•
Complete predicate			•	•
Subject or predicate, difficult to identify			•	•
Direct object/compound direct object			•	•
Indirect object			•	•
Object pronouns as indirect/direct objects			•	•
Predicate noun/predicate adjective			•	•
Simple sentence	•	•	•	•
Compound sentence	•	•	•	•
Complex sentence/dependent clause			•	•
Adjective clause				•
Adverb clause				•
PARAGRAPHS				
Paragraphs and compositions	•	•	•	•
Suggestions for writing a paragraph	•	•	•	•
LETTERS				
Friendly letter: parts	•	•	•	•
Friendly letter: capitalization/punctuation	•	•	•	•
Business letter: parts	•	•	•	•
Business letter: greeting/close/signature			•	•
Business letter: capitalization/punctuation/ postal codes	•	•	•	•
Envelope	•	•	•	•
USING A DICTIONARY				
Dictionary: introduction	•	•	•	•
Dictionary: alphabetical order	•	•	•	•
Syllables			•	•
Word division—introduction	•	•	•	•
Word division—rules			•	•
Respelling for pronunciation	•	•	•	•
Spelling	•	•	•	•
SPEAKING AND LISTENING				
Speaking	•	•	•	•
Listening	•	•	•	•

Student Book Organization

The *Practical Guide to Better English* **Student Book** for each level includes the following elements and features:

INSTRUCTION

- 72 one-page grammar/usage/mechanics *instructional lessons*—nine per unit.

- 8 two-page *composition lessons*—one per unit.

- 8 one-page grammar/usage/mechanics *unit reviews*—one per unit.

CUMULATIVE REVIEW

- A year-end review unit consisting of 9 one-page grammar/usage/mechanics *review lessons* and a final two-page *cumulative review*.

HANDBOOK RESOURCE

- A *Handbook of grammar, usage, and mechanics rules* organized topically into 45 Guides.

- *Practice activities* following each Handbook section, for each principle explained in the Handbook.

Each lesson directs students to the appropriate Guide or Guides in the Handbook for explicit instruction in grammar, usage, and mechanics principles. In addition, an alphabetical index to topics covered in the Handbook is included at the end of the book.

WORD STUDY

- *Vocabulary puzzlers* of various kinds build students' knowledge of word structure, word meanings, and word relationships.

CORRELATION OF HANDBOOK GUIDES TO LESSONS

HANDBOOK GUIDE	LESSONS
1 Sentences	1, 2, 8, 9, 11, 14, 22, 26, 31, 33, 42, 53, 64, 75, 86, 89, 97, 98
2 Capitalization	3, 4, 11, 14, 22, 26, 33, 42, 47, 53, 64, 75, 86, 97, 98
Capitalization/Punctuation	
3 Initials of Names	4, 7, 53, 64, 75
4 Titles with Names	4, 7, 26, 42, 45, 55, 64
5 Days of Week	7, 11
6 Months of Year	7, 11
7 Addresses	5, 7, 8, 11, 24, 26, 31, 33, 53, 98
8 Titles	42, 53, 64, 75, 97, 98
9 Quotations	14, 15, 22, 26, 31, 33, 42, 53, 64, 75, 86, 92, 97, 98
Other Uses of Commas	
10 Dates	53, 75, 97, 98
11 Direct Address	5, 8, 11, 22, 31, 53, 64, 75, 86, 97
12 *Yes* and *No*	5, 8, 11, 22, 31, 42, 53, 58, 64, 75, 86, 97, 98
13 Words in Series/ Compound Sentences	5, 8, 11, 31, 42, 75, 86, 97, 98
14 **Contractions**	17, 22, 42, 58, 64, 66, 74, 75, 81, 86, 91, 97, 98
15 **Nouns**	27, 33, 34
16 Singular & Plural Forms	28, 33, 91, 98
17 Possessive Forms	29, 31, 33, 42, 58, 64, 66, 75, 91, 98
18 **Pronouns**	34, 35, 36, 37, 38, 40, 44, 56, 60, 61, 66, 74, 85, 95, 98
19 **Verbs**	6, 11
20 Singular & Plural Forms	6, 11, 17, 22, 56, 66, 74, 81, 85, 94
21 Principal Parts	19, 20, 21, 22, 56, 66, 74, 85, 87, 94, 98
22 **Adjectives**	73, 77, 80, 88
23 **Adverbs**	73, 77, 80, 88
24 **Conjunctions**	78, 79, 80, 88
Word Study	
25 Homophones	50, 55, 59, 66, 72, 93, 98
26 Synonyms	70, 71, 77, 93, 98
27 Antonyms	71, 77, 93, 98
28 **Paragraphs**	10, 12, 13, 21, 25, 32, 39, 40, 43, 54, 63, 65, 76, 80, 87, 88
29 **Speaking & Listening**	(Oral language development is supported throughout lessons.)
Writing Letters	
30 Friendly Letter	23, 25
31 Business Letter	46, 47, 48, 55, 90
32 Envelope Address	24, 33
Troublesome Words and Expressions	
33 *Teach* and *Learn*	16, 22, 56, 74, 85, 94, 98
34 *Lie* and *Lay*	51, 52, 55, 56, 66, 74, 94, 98
35 *May* and *Can*	16, 22, 56
36 *Sit* and *Set*	62, 66, 74, 94, 98
37 *Doesn't* and *Don't*	74, 85, 94, 98
38 *Into* and *In*	74
39 Double Negatives	18, 22, 74, 84, 94
40 Unnecessary Words	41, 44, 84
41 Expressions to Be Avoided	61, 84, 85, 94
42 **Using a Dictionary**	68, 69, 77
43 Alphabetical Order/Spelling	67, 68, 69, 77, 96, 98
44 Division of Words	49, 55, 68, 69, 77, 88, 96
45 Sentence Structure	30, 33, 57, 82, 83, 95, 98

Teacher's Guide Organization

The *Practical Guide to Better English* **Teacher's Guide** for each level includes the following resources for teaching and managing the program:

OVERVIEW
- **Overviews** of the program, the student book, and the teacher's guide.

SCOPE AND SEQUENCE
- **Scope and Sequence Chart** of the grammar, usage, and mechanics skills taught in each level.

CORRELATION
- **Correlation** between the Handbook topics and individual lessons for that level.

PROCEDURES
- A **description of the five-step process of teaching a unit:** administering the diagnostic test; presenting each individual skill lesson; teaching the writing lesson; using the review lesson; and administering the achievement test.

- A **description of the basic sequence for presenting a lesson:** introducing the skill; directing students to the instructional text; previewing the content; assigning the lesson items; checking answers; assigning additional activities; and reviewing the lesson.

- **Suggestions for introducing the program** to students.

- **Descriptions of instructional procedures and options for meeting students' individual needs:** tips for classroom management; for promoting oral language development; for teaching composition; for adapting lessons to meet students' individual needs; and for helping students who are acquiring English.

- **Procedures and materials for evaluation of student progress:** suggested informal and formal assessment methods; reproducible blackline masters of diagnostic and achievement tests for each unit; a reproducible record-keeping form for tracking individual progress; and a rubric and checklists for use in evaluating the writing lessons.

ANSWER KEYS
- **Answer keys** for diagnostic and achievement tests and for student book lessons.

INDEX
- **Index of topical content** of individual lessons in the student book for that level.

How to Teach a Unit

Level II of *Practical Guide to Better English* includes eight instructional units and a final review unit. The units are developmental and are intended to be taught in the order in which they are presented. Nevertheless, it is entirely appropriate to present lessons—or units—in any order that fits with your instructional goals. Each lesson in the program can stand alone because each is fully supported by instructions in the Handbook.

Each unit will take about three weeks to teach. The pace can easily be slowed or accelerated, however, to fit with students' progress.

Practical Guide to Better English
UNIT PLANNER
Option 1: Daily Practice

	MONDAY	TUESDAY	WEDNESDAY	THURSDAY	FRIDAY
Week 1	Diagnostic Test	Lesson 1	Lesson 2	Lesson 3	Lesson 4
Week 2	Lesson 5	Lesson 6	Lesson 7	Lesson 8	Lesson 9
Week 3	Composition Planning and Writing	Composition Revision	Composition Presentation	Review Lesson	Achievement Test

Practical Guide to Better English
UNIT PLANNER
Option 2: Three-Day-a-Week Practice

	MONDAY	TUESDAY	WEDNESDAY	THURSDAY	FRIDAY
Week 1	Diagnostic Test/ Lesson 1		Lesson 2		Lesson 3
Week 2	Lesson 4		Lesson 5		Lesson 6
Week 3	Lesson 7		Lesson 8		Lesson 9
Week 4	Composition Planning and Writing		Composition Revision and Presentation/ Review Lesson		Achievement Test

The recommended procedure for teaching a unit involves these five steps:

1. Administer the diagnostic test.

The diagnostic test for each unit can be used to measure what students know at the *beginning* of a unit. The diagnostic test should be administered before students begin working on the unit skill lessons. Students' performance on a diagnostic test can be compared with their performance on the achievement test, given at the end of the unit. Reproducible masters for the diagnostic tests begin on page 24 of this teacher's guide. A reproducible record-keeping form for the diagnostic and achievement tests is included on page 60.

2. Present each individual skill lesson.

Each unit contains nine skill lessons. It is recommended that one lesson be taught each day. Suggested procedures for presenting a lesson appear in the next section of this teacher's guide. The time required to teach a particular lesson will vary according to the difficulty of the concept, the nature of the practice, the instructional procedures used, and the students' ability.

3. Teach the writing lesson.

Each instructional unit contains a two-page writing lesson following the regular skill lessons. These activities lead students step-by-step through the task of writing and revising original compositions. A writing lesson can be completed in two or three class periods, depending on the available time and the students' writing proficiency. Each writing lesson has been designed so that students can complete it independently; however, some students may need additional guidance. Suggested procedures for presenting the writing lessons appear on pages 18–19 of this teacher's guide. A rubric for evaluating compositions and checklists for scoring the writing lessons can be found on pages 61-65.

4. Assign the review lesson.

A review lesson at the end of each instructional unit briefly covers the skills and concepts taught in the lessons. The review lesson is designed to reinforce learning and also indicate areas in which students may need remediation. Class time remaining after administering and checking the review lesson should be used to provide students with help on the skills they have not fully grasped, which should include careful review of the Handbook sections that instruct those skills.

5. Administer the achievement test.

At the conclusion of each unit, a two-page achievement test should be administered to all students. Reproducible masters for the achievement tests begin on page 26 of this teacher's guide. Students' performance on this test can be compared with their performance on the diagnostic test to measure progress. The reproducible record-keeping form on page 60 of this guide may be used to keep track of student progress. For more information on assessment procedures and options, see "Assessment" on pages 22–23 of this teacher's guide.

How to Present a Lesson

Each unit in Level II of *Practical Guide to Better English* includes nine skill lessons. All lessons have a common structure that allows for as much or as little teacher guidance as a teacher chooses to provide.

The teaching procedure outlined here calls for teacher guidance throughout the lesson. Although it requires more time and direct involvement, this procedure offers a number of benefits: more opportunities for oral language development, effective use of scaffolding, modeling of correct English usage, constructive feedback, and authentic ongoing assessment. This procedure is especially recommended for use in the first few weeks of the school term, and whenever challenging new grammar concepts are being introduced.

If teacher involvement is impractical, students can be directed to complete the skill lessons independently. *All lessons in this program are written to be self-directing.* In addition, the Handbook serves as a dependable source of information for students working on their own. The more students use the Handbook as a resource, the better prepared they will be for success on the job, where the ability to use information in a manual or a handbook is a key to advancement.

Additional suggestions for presenting skill lessons are included in the sections of this teacher's guide that focus on managing classrooms, developing oral language, adapting lessons to meet individual needs, and helping students who are acquiring English.

RECOMMENDED SEQUENCE

1. **Introduce the skill.** Read the lesson title aloud. Engage students by asking questions that will help them make connections to previous lessons and prior knowledge. For example, for the lesson entitled "Punctuating Sentences," you might ask, *"What punctuation marks have you already studied? Which of these are used at the end of a sentence? What other punctuation marks are used at the end of a sentence?"*

2. **Direct students to the instructional text.** Point out the Handbook Guide(s) listed in the gray box. If a rule statement is given in the box, ask a volunteer to read it aloud. Next, have students find the guide(s) in their Handbooks, read the instructional text, complete the practice items, and check their answers. (If the practice items have been completed previously, have students review just the rules and the examples.) Students who are unable to complete the Handbook

practice items successfully may need special help before they begin working on the lesson.

3. **Preview the content.** Discuss with students the lesson topic. This can be determined by skimming the exercise sentences. The "Index of Topics Featured in Level II" at the end of this teacher's guide may also be used to identify the topic. Invite students to share what they already know about the topic. For example, for the lesson that tells about the rodeo known as the Calgary Stampede, you might ask: *"What do you already know about rodeos?" Have any of you seen a rodeo or competed in one? What are some of the events in a rodeo? What skills do those events require? Have you heard of a rodeo called the Calgary Stampede? Where is the city of Calgary? What is a stampede?"* By helping students focus on the content topic and building their background knowledge, you increase the likelihood that they will read the lesson items with good comprehension and become engaged with the language and content of the lesson.

4. **Assign the items.** Read aloud the instructions. Invite a volunteer to copy the example items on the chalkboard. Read aloud the items, describe how you would decide on the correct response, and model how you would write your response on the board. Then ask students to complete the lesson items independently or with partners.

5. **Check answers.** Invite volunteers to give their responses to the items orally; have students check their own work. Use the lesson answer key at the end of this teacher's guide to verify that responses given by students are correct. Invite students to ask questions about items they found difficult or confusing.

6. **Assign the additional section or vocabulary activity.** If the lesson has a Part II activity or a vocabulary puzzler, read aloud the instructions for it and discuss any examples. Next, have students complete the activity independently or with a partner. Then have volunteers give their answers while students check their own work. For those Part II activities that ask students to write original sentences, you may want to evaluate responses yourself.

7. **Review the lesson.** Have students count their correct responses and record their score at the top of the page and also on the score chart on page 176 of their books. Then invite one student to restate the rules and concepts learned in the lesson and tell how he or she can put these to use in writing and speaking.

Introducing the Program to Students

Teachers report that high school and adult students generally work more productively in courses in which the goals, instructional focus, procedures, and benefits are outlined in advance. Accordingly, you may want to use the following sequence to introduce *Practical Guide to Better English* to students.

1. Preview. Invite students to preview the book and talk about what they notice. Point out the goal statement at the beginning of "A Note to Students," which appears before the Contents page.

2. Set goals. Ask students to suggest reasons why it is important to be able to speak and write effectively using correct English. Record their reasons on the chalkboard. Then suggest to students that they choose one or more of these reasons as their personal goals and write these on a sheet of paper.

3. Look at one lesson. Have students all turn to one instructional lesson, such as Lesson 6, on page 10 of their books. Point out the *lesson title*, which gives the skill focus. Then point out the shaded box with the *listing of Handbook Guides*. Explain that these Handbook Guides have the rules and information they will need to learn in order to complete the lessons. Point out that the box also contains a rule reminder. Next, point out the instructions for the lesson and the examples of how to complete the items. Finally, point out the numbered *lesson items* and the *vocabulary puzzler* entitled "Name That Job."

4. Look at the Handbook. Explain to students that the Handbook is a reference they can use to learn and check what is correct English. Remind students that each lesson has a listing of the Handbook Guides they will need to study for that lesson. Have them turn to the Handbook Guides listed for Lesson 6— Guides 19 and 20. Have volunteers read aloud the guides and orally complete the practice items. Then point out the answers; explain to students that as they read the guide sections, they should complete the practice items and check their answers to make sure they understand the rules.

5. Model the procedure for completing a lesson independently. Have a volunteer read aloud the steps for completing the lessons on page 2 of the student book. After each step is read, describe how you would carry this out for Lesson 6.

6. Look at one writing lesson. Explain to students that in addition to learning the rules of written English, they will have several opportunities to put the rules into action by writing their own compositions. Inform them that there are eight writing lessons in the book, and that each one teaches a particular kind of writing.

Introduce the writing lessons by having students turn to Lesson 32 of Unit III, "Writing a Problem/Solution Paragraph," on pages 38–39. Point out the *lesson title*. Then point out the bulleted list of *tips*. Explain that each writing lesson has a list of guidelines for the type of writing focused on in the lesson. Direct students' attention to the *writing model* and explain that it is an example of the writing form. As they write their own paragraph, they can look at the model for help. Finally, point out the heading *Write a Problem/Solution Paragraph* on page 39. Explain that these sections guide them through the steps of writing a paragraph. Point out that they will write their paragraph on another piece of paper.

7. Discuss assessment procedures. Explain to students that they will take a test at the beginning and end of each unit. The diagnostic test at the beginning of each unit will indicate what they already know about the skills and rules that will be taught in the unit. The achievement test at the end of each unit will show what they have learned. Then tell students that in addition to the test the following activities will be evaluated: the sentences and paragraphs they write; how well they are able to revise and correct their work; how effectively they speak and listen; and their scores on the instructional lessons and review lessons.

Explain that these assessments can help identify concepts and rules they don't fully understand and skills they have not yet mastered. Assure students that you will work with them to help them master the skills and concepts that initially cause them problems.

Tips for Classroom Management

The *Practical Guide to Better English* program requires minimal teacher direction. As a result, it helps solve classroom management problems rather than create them. *All lessons in the program are self-instructive*, so students can be directed to work independently, or in pairs or small groups, while you work with the rest of the class on another task. The self-instructive nature of the lessons, plus the support for independent learning provided by the Handbook, allow for great flexibility in pacing and grouping, as described in the following sections.

Flexibility. The program provides a year's course of study. Lessons are developmental, and spiral learning occurs within and across levels to reinforce concepts and skills. The program can be easily adapted to suit the needs of individual classrooms because *every skill lesson can stand alone*. The Handbook Guides referenced in each lesson provide students with the concepts and rules they need to complete the lesson successfully. Further, since the Handbook itself is organized in sensible sequence to explain grammar, usage, and mechanics concepts, students who find themselves unsure of how a particular rule fits in the greater fabric of correct English can read the Handbook Guide sections before and after the sections referenced to gain a better understanding.

As you use this level of *Practical Guide to Better English* in your classroom, feel free to expand, drop, or change the order of lessons. Your sense of what will be of greatest value to your students is the best guide to what lessons should be taught when.

Pacing. Because the skill lessons in *Practical Guide to Better English* are self-instructive and free-standing, the program offers more pacing options than comparable programs. Among these options are the following:

- The whole class can proceed at a single pace.

- Students can be grouped heterogeneously, and all groups can proceed at a similar pace.

- Students can be grouped homogeneously, and each group can proceed at a pace appropriate for its members.

- Students who need work on all skills and concepts can work through the program together at a steady pace. Students who have greater proficiency can work on just those lessons that focus on problems that show up in their written work.

- All students can work at their own pace, checking in with you each time they are ready to begin or conclude a unit.

Grouping. Most students will benefit from working with other students at least part of the time. Group work offers opportunities for oral language development, cooperative problem-solving, peer tutoring and counseling, shared reading, and oral presentation of written work to an audience. Each mode offers particular advantages:

- Working in *small heterogeneous groups* allows students with less advanced literacy skills to benefit from the modeling and mentoring of more proficient students. In turn, the more proficient students develop communications skills and strengthen their own knowledge of grammar, usage, and mechanics principles as they work to convey these concepts to others in the group.

- Working in *small homogeneous groups* offers greater opportunities for providing scaffolding. (See "Adapting Lessons to Meet Students' Individual Needs" on pages 20–21 of this teacher's guide.) Many teachers report that students are most comfortable and work most productively in groups in which other students have the same level of proficiency. In part this may be because members of such groups can all contribute to the problem-solving process— none of them has all the answers.

- Working in *pairs* encourages thought and dialogue. Many of the skills activities in the lessons in *Practical Guide to Better English* lend themselves to partnered learning. Pairs of students working on the same lesson can share prior knowledge of the skill and the lesson topic, and read and discuss the Handbook Guides together. They can work independently on the exercise items, and then reconvene to check answers and help each other clear up any areas of confusion.

Promoting Oral Language Development

The process of acquiring English language skills begins with oral language development. Students need to hear correct language patterns, and practice producing these in their own speech, in order to internalize the patterns and employ them in their writing.

Oral communication is of particular benefit to students with limited fluency and knowledge of the English language because it allows them to experiment with language in a setting that is less formal and less threatening than written formats. At the same time, oral language activities—listening as well as speaking—expand students' vocabularies, which is essential for their educational progress and eventual success in the working world.

In order to develop oral language skills, students should have opportunities to do these things:

- Listen and speak for a **variety of purposes**: give directions, seek information, express opinions, respond to requests.

- Listen to and contribute ideas **in various settings**: one-to-one, small-group, and whole-class discussions.

- Listen and speak to share **knowledge about lesson topics.**

- Listen to and read aloud **models of basic grammatical structures** in order to gain oral fluency using proper syntax.

- Listen to and repeat **accurate pronunciation of words** in order to achieve effective oral communication.

- Listen to and discuss the **differences between formal and informal language** and the settings in which each is appropriate.

- Listen to and repeat examples of the **diversity of language** and recognize how it is used for different purposes and audiences in various types of communication.

The instructional skill lessons in *Practical Guide to Better English* offer many opportunities for listening and speaking:

- When a skill lesson is first presented, students can **share knowledge and opinions about the lesson topics.**

- During the lesson introduction, students can **read aloud rule statements, discuss examples, suggest other examples orally, or complete the Handbook practice activities orally.**

- As the class prepares to complete the skill lesson, students can **read aloud the instructions or the lesson sentences.**

- After students complete the lesson, they can **give correct answers orally and explain how they decided that they were correct.**

- Prior to completing open-ended exercise items (writing sentences with a certain grammatical element, combining sentences, and so on), students can **read aloud the items and discuss possible responses to each.**

- If the lesson offers a vocabulary extension activity, students can **solve the vocabulary puzzler orally.**

- As an extension activity, students inspired by the topic of a particular lesson can **prepare and present brief oral reports.**

The writing lessons also offer opportunities for productive oral expression:

- When a writing form is introduced, students can **share what they know** about that form and discuss any writing or reading experiences they may have had with that type of writing.

- Students can **read the writing model aloud** and share their reactions. For instance, after reading a persuasive paragraph, they might give their own opinions about the issue. After reading a science report, they might share other facts they know about the topic.

- Students can **orally answer the questions** that ask them to identify specific elements in the model.

- As they plan their own writing, students can work cooperatively to **brainstorm topic ideas** or **discuss the sequence of ideas** that might work best for expository or narrative compositions.

- Revising written work offers students the opportunity to **give and receive constructive feedback**: students can trade drafts and **offer suggestions** for revision.

- Students can **read aloud their completed writing;** listeners can **give their reactions**.

- Process writing lessons also offer students multiple opportunities for oral expression as they **brainstorm, revise,** and **publish** their work.

Teaching Composition

The writing component of *Practical Guide to Better English* offers students the opportunity to apply grammar, usage, and mechanics skills in the context of original compositions. Authentic writing activities ask students to draw upon their own experiences, opinions, interests, and ideas, as well as factual information from the content areas. They can use these experiences as they learn to construct paragraphs, essays, reports, narratives, and other standard forms of writing required for success in school, on state assessment tests, in daily life, and in the workplace.

The Domains of Writing. The domains of writing are generally (although not universally) identified as **expository, persuasive, narrative,** and **descriptive.** The writing lessons in *Practical Guide to Better English* reflect the writing requirements and domains currently in use in many states across the country. The lessons are designed to help students understand that each form of writing has its own purpose, audience, and structure. The forms listed in the chart below are taught in the *Practical Guide to Better English* writing lessons.

Program Goals. The writing exercises and lessons of *Practical Guide to Better English* are designed to help students develop writing fluency at the sentence, paragraph, and whole composition levels. The program is developmental in nature, beginning with simple tasks and progressing to more challenging ones—both within and across grade levels. The lessons are designed to help students develop these skills:

- Write in a variety of circumstances: in response to questions that require single-sentence answers; to writing prompts that require a response of one or more paragraphs; and to longer, more formal assignments.

- Use the steps of the writing process.

- Revise writing based on feedback and reflection.

- Use the conventions of grammar and spelling, and develop good proofreading habits.

- Write for real-life situations: college or job applications, letters, resumes, and so on.

Process Writing vs. Demand Writing. Of the eight writing lessons presented in each level of *Practical Guide to Better English*, two take students through the steps of the writing process. The other six lessons guide students in developing shorter compositions, what some researchers call *demand writing*. Demand writing requires students to develop a clear, cohesive response to a specific writing prompt, in a controlled setting, often in a limited amount of time. Preparation for statewide writing proficiency tests is one good reason to teach demand writing; another is its wealth of real-life applications. As adults, students will engage in demand writing in most cases when writing is required—when composing letters, filling out job applications, giving directions and explanations, and in many other everyday tasks.

The writing lessons in Units IV and VIII teach students a useful method for developing longer, more complex compositions, such as research reports, essays, and narratives.

EXPOSITORY	PERSUASIVE	NARRATIVE	DESCRIPTIVE
compare/contrast (III)	**persuasive paragraph** (I, II, III)	**personal narrative** (I, II, III)	descriptive sentences (I)
research report (I, III)	**persuasive essay** (IV)	**story—narrative elements** (I, II, IV)	descriptive paragraph (I, II)
summary (I, III)	product endorsement (III)		descriptive composition (III)
how-to paragraph (I, II)	résumé (IV)		descriptive essay (IV)
problem/solution (II, IV)	**letter of application for employment** (IV)		
paragraph of information (II)			
explanation (II, IV)			
biography (III)			
news articles (III)			

(Assignments that appear in boldface type are presented as process writing activities at least once in the program. Numbers in parentheses indicate at which level[s] the writing form is taught.)

TEACHING THE WRITING LESSONS

Each writing lesson is designed so that students can complete it independently. However, some students may need additional support. Here are some suggestions for adapting the writing lessons for students with differing needs:

Students Acquiring English. In the sequence of language acquisition, writing fluency is usually the last skill second-language learners acquire. When teaching composition to students acquiring English, help them develop ideas and try out sentence structures by offering opportunities for oral language expression before, during, and after writing. (See the section entitled "Promoting Oral Language Development" in this teacher's guide for oral language opportunities in the writing lessons.)

Here are some additional procedures that can help second-language learners:

- **Determine students' writing fluency in their native language.** Ask students to describe writing they have done. Have them describe the processes they use when they write. (Example: *If you wanted to compare a lion and a tiger, how would you do it in writing?*) If students possess writing fluency in their native language, they are likely to need less instruction on the structure of the various writing forms taught in this program.

- **Provide support with syntax.** Students acquiring English are likely to struggle with usage issues such as subject-verb agreement, pronoun use, article use, verb forms, and sentence structure. Have students identify and tag the Handbook Guides that focus on these, and remind them to refer to those sections often. In addition, you may need to assign specific usage lessons a second time.

- **Pair each second-language learner with a partner who is fluent in English.** Have the partner read aloud the writing model, and have the student acquiring English retell it orally. Partners can then discuss the writing assignment together and talk about what they plan to write. The second-language learner can dictate his or her paragraph(s). Partners should work together to proofread and correct their work.

Students with Little or No Writing Experience. Students with limited writing experience often have little idea of how to begin a writing assignment; they also typically do not know what is expected in terms of the product. Group these students *homogeneously* and go through the first several writing assignments with them, modeling how you would complete each step. Then walk students through the lesson again, this time having students complete the various parts of the writing activity as a group. It is particularly important for these students to spend time thinking about how the writing model is structured because they bring little knowledge with them about the organization and purpose of different writing forms. As students gain confidence as writers and familiarity with the various domains, gradually encourage them to tackle the writing lessons in pairs or independently.

Students with Poor Reading Fluency. Some students who are poor readers can be quite successful at writing, with guidance and encouragement. It may benefit these students to complete the writing activities with a *peer partner* who has good reading skills, but may be a less fluent writer or inventive thinker. That student can read the tips, writing model, and instructions aloud, and the partners can help each other plan and write their paragraphs.

Reluctant Writers. Students who display a reluctance to write may be encouraged to begin by writing only a small amount—perhaps just one sentence. You may need to work with these students *individually*. Encourage all efforts, no matter how minimal the outcome may seem: one sentence is a beginning! Gradually, encourage students to add sentences until they are composing complete paragraphs. Alternately, you might put off teaching the writing lessons until later in the year, when students' writing fluency at the sentence level has increased and their confidence as writers has improved.

Special Help for Nonproductive Writers. Students who possess little writing fluency frequently feel intimidated by even simple writing tasks, and often bring with them years of frustration and discouragement. Here are some additional suggestions for helping these students:

- Praise students' attempts, especially at the beginning. Point out strengths in their written work *before* helping them find areas that need improvement. Assure students that their writing will improve, and that writing is a skill that takes time and practice to learn.

- Guide students to see that *writing is a process that begins with thinking*, and help them learn organizational strategies that allow them to collect their thoughts before they write.

- Often, a composition that is weak in many ways nonetheless contains one element that is particularly praiseworthy: a descriptive phrase that is especially colorful; a unique word choice; a powerful or moving sentence about an event. Look for these "unexpected gems" and share them with the class. Reading these passages aloud will demonstrate some elements of good writing and boost the confidence of less fluent writers. Try to read from every student's work at least once. Telling students that any student work that is read aloud will be read anonymously will help them feel comfortable with this practice.

- Start slowly, and build over time. Adapt the sequence and complexity of writing activities to match your students' abilities. Move from sentence to paragraph to composition slowly, recognizing that different students will progress at different paces. When students do show increased fluency and confidence, though, be sure to offer them writing assignments that challenge them appropriately, while providing the support they will need to succeed on these. (See "Adapting Lessons to Meet Students' Individual Needs" in this teacher's guide for a discussion of scaffolding.)

EVALUATION AND ASSESSMENT

Establishing a Baseline. At the beginning of the school year you may wish to establish the baseline proficiency of the students in your class. This will help you assess individual students' strengths and weaknesses, and may help you employ grouping strategies that will help your students grow as writers. To establish a baseline, give all students the same writing prompt to respond to. The prompt should not require any specialized knowledge or vocabulary. (Example: *What is your earliest memory? Write about it.*) Responses will give you an indication of each student's writing fluency. Compare this initial assignment with subsequent writing efforts to help you assess progress.

Using a Rubric and Checklists to Evaluate Writing. A rubric that can be used to help you evaluate the overall quality of students' compositions has been provided on page 61 of this teacher's guide. Evaluation checklists, which have been provided for each writing lesson in the student book, begin on page

62 of this teacher's guide. It is recommended that you duplicate a set of these checklists for each student at the beginning of the year; they will serve as both evaluation and record-keeping forms.

Student Self-Evaluation. Periodically, have students compare their early work with their later writing so that they, too, can be aware of their growth as writers. You may choose occasionally to have more fluent writers use the checklists to evaluate their own work. Alternately, have more advanced students construct their own criteria by asking them questions such as: *What makes an outstanding personal narrative?* Encourage students to use their criteria as guides when evaluating their own work and the work of their peers.

REMEDIATION AND PRACTICE

Grammar and Mechanics. Most developing writers need ongoing practice with basic grammar and mechanics skills, such as avoiding run-ons and sentence fragments, using high-utility homophones such as *it's* and *its* properly, and using commas correctly. As you identify specific skills that need improvement, assign one or more of the following remediation activities:

- Have students review the appropriate section(s) of the Handbook and study the practice exercises. Give them five additional practice items to complete for each skill.

- Have students complete a lesson that focuses on the targeted skill a second time. Repeat this until students can answer each item correctly.

- Help students create a list of their own "trouble spots," including references to the Handbook Guides, and use the list whenever they revise their writing. As they achieve mastery with specific skills, they can remove those "trouble spots" from the list.

Content. Developing writers often struggle with organizing and sequencing the flow of their ideas. Help them to see writing as a thinking process. Visual mapping activities such as word webs, outlines, and Venn diagrams can help students organize their thoughts and understand the vital connection between thinking and writing. If possible, evaluate completed writing with students individually. Help them identify ideas that are repeated, contradictory, out of sequence, or off the topic. Then have students rewrite the piece, based on their own observations.

Practice. Following are some suggestions for helping students practice their writing and revising skills outside the lessons:

- Provide additional writing prompts to reinforce demand writing skills. Encourage students to make a habit of using the *Plan* and *Write* steps to help them organize their thoughts quickly before they begin writing.

- Have students rewrite exercise sentences from an instructional lesson as paragraphs, adding transition words, an introduction, and a conclusion. Encourage them to consider resequencing the sentences to improve the flow of ideas.

- To provide proofreading practice, pair students and have each one rewrite a paragraph from a book, omitting all punctuation and capitalization and inserting some spelling errors. Partners can trade passages, correct them, and then check their work against the original passage.

Adapting Lessons to Meet Students' Individual Needs

Students learn best when lessons encourage them to stretch for new knowledge *that is within their reach if they stretch.* This process of having to work to grasp a concept ensures engagement, develops thinking processes, and prepares the student for the next stretch he or she will need to make.

Education researchers, such as Dr. Robert Rueda of the University of Southern California, have explained the process of supporting students' learning as being similar to constructing **scaffolding**. The best kind of help puts each student within reach—but not always easy reach—of important concepts and information.

What makes this process challenging for a teacher are the many differences among students in any class. Students bring with them widely differing literacy skills and background knowledge; they learn in different ways, and they learn at different paces. Adjusting each lesson to provide just the right amount of challenge to each student is a goal unlikely to be met in a real-world classroom.

Nevertheless, you can make instruction significantly more effective by keeping in mind the effectiveness of scaffolding and becoming aware of students' preferred modes of learning and varying levels of proficiency.

ADDRESSING THE THREE MODALITIES

Over the years many teachers have found it helpful to tailor some activities to students who learn best *visually,* some to students who learn best *aurally,* and some to students who learn best *kinesthetically.* Lessons in *Practical Guide to Better English* can be adapted in a number of ways to address each of these modalities. Here are a few suggestions:

Visual. As a part of each lesson on sentence structure, show students how to diagram a simple sentence with that structure. Diagramming was formerly thought of by some as tedious and esoteric; and it can be, with complex sentences. But a sentence diagram is actually a graphic organizer—a highly visual way of illustrating how basic sentence elements relate to one another. Showing students how to diagram simple sentences is likely to be of great help to those who are visual learners.

Aural. In lessons on parts of speech and on related word forms, read aloud lesson sentences using nonsense substitutions to highlight functions and inflected endings.

The *bink binked* a *bink.*

The *bink binked binkly.*

The *binky bink* was *binked* by a *bink.*

Students can be asked to replace the nonsense forms with real words, and explain how they decided what kind of word to use.

Kinesthetic. To help students understand how different parts of speech and kinds of phrases function in sentences, have students cut sentences from the lesson apart into words and phrases, and then see how many sentences *different from the originals* they can put together using clear tape.

ADAPTING LESSONS FOR STUDENTS WITH LESS PROFICIENCY

Users of this program are likely to have already developed a number of effective ways to help less advanced students gain benefit from lessons they are unable to complete independently. Following are some suggestions that may or may not be new to you.

- Read Handbook sections, lesson directions, and any examples aloud. Have a volunteer write the first lesson item on the board and model completing it. Then have students work in pairs to complete the lesson items.

- Have students work in a small group led by a peer tutor. Group members can take turns completing items, showing their responses to the group, and explaining their answer choices.

- Using the chalkboard, model completing the first five items of a lesson. Have students watch with their books closed. Then have them open their books and work on those same five items, plus the next five. Have them then stop, check, and discuss their work. Finally, have them complete the remaining items.

- For the first item, write a correct response and an incorrect response on the chalkboard. Have students raise their hands when you point to the response they believe is correct. Ask a student who identified the correct response to tell why it is correct. Continue this process until students seem confident they can complete the remaining items independently.

Helping Students Who Are Acquiring English

Older students who are acquiring English face a special challenge. The content load of the texts for which they are responsible in classes or on the job is typically heavy, but their oral and written English skills may be at a relatively low level. Yet they have a compelling need to understand and make use of the information in such texts because long-term success in the workplace depends on their being able to do so.

For these students to have the best possible chance of succeeding in a course of study, both the materials and the instruction must be considerate of their needs and abilities. Simplicity and clarity are extremely important. As Robert Rueda, professor of educational psychology at the University of Southern California has written, "Trying to learn difficult academic content at the same time one is trying to understand an unfamiliar language tends to overload the capacity to learn."

The lessons and Handbook Guides in the *Practical Guide to Better English* program have been written and structured to meet the needs of second language learners and their teachers. Every effort has been made to simplify language and structure and eliminate obstacles to understanding. Nevertheless, because the program deals with a complex subject—the structure and rules of the English language—students acquiring English are likely to experience some language-related difficulties in the course of completing lessons. Your ability to recognize that a student is having difficulty and offer appropriate help is one of the most important elements in the instructional process. The teaching procedures listed below have been shown to be of significant value to second language learners, both in helping them complete coursework successfully and in advancing their acquisition of English.

ORAL LANGUAGE DEVELOPMENT

- Read aloud examples and answers.

- Ask students to answer items orally.

- Model effective oral reading and pronunciation by reading passages aloud.

- Use repetition—have students repeat what they hear.

- For those students with lesser levels of English proficiency, have them respond orally to questions whose answers they have already learned.

VOCABULARY DEVELOPMENT

- Identify and review key vocabulary and concepts for exercises; write these words on the chalkboard; use pictures or props to illustrate word meanings when possible.

- Discuss the meanings of unfamiliar expressions and idioms.

- Discuss troublesome words: multiple meaning words, homophones, and homographs. Guide students to use context to determine meaning.

- Direct students to develop webs of related words for use in writing activities.

- Encourage students to keep lists of words they want to make part of their active vocabulary; encourage them to use these in class discussions and writing activities.

CONCEPT DEVELOPMENT AND SKILL INSTRUCTION (SCAFFOLDING)

- Activate students' prior knowledge of familiar subjects through class discussion.

- Discuss with students topics likely to be unfamiliar to them before directing them to read or write about those topics.

- Read aloud and model activities with volunteers.

- Redefine terms orally.

- Speak clearly and pause often.

- Say the same thing in different ways.

- Ask yes/no questions to engage students.

- Use visual learning cues—drawings, photographs, illustrations—when possible.

- Dramatize meaning through facial expressions, pantomime, and gestures.

- Check comprehension frequently by asking questions.

- Remind students of particular things to do or avoid doing.

- Have students dictate their ideas for writing activities before they begin the task of writing.

- Encourage students to make comparisons between their primary language and English.

COOPERATIVE LEARNING

- Have students work with English-proficient partners on proofreading activities.

- Offer opportunities for students who share the same primary language to work on skill lessons and activities together.

AWARENESS OF CULTURAL DIFFERENCES

- Be prepared for different personal responses to exercise items.

- Keep in mind that students' difficulties in responding to a lesson topic may be the result of cultural differences rather than lack of comprehension of vocabulary.

Assessment

A cornerstone of the *Practical Guide to Better English* program is ongoing assessment that provides a clear picture of each student's level of proficiency with specific English language skills and writing tasks. The program's formal assessment instruments enable you to adjust instruction in each unit to fit students' needs as well as monitor their progress. Informal assessment, which can take many forms, including those outlined on the next page, provides additional information about students' strengths and weaknesses. Assessment of the writing activities enables both teachers and students to recognize growth in language proficiency as well as identify areas in which more work is needed.

FORMAL ASSESSMENT IN *PRACTICAL GUIDE TO BETTER ENGLISH*

Diagnostic Tests. Each unit's diagnostic test provides a quick snapshot of students' familiarity with the skills covered in that unit. Reproducible masters of diagnostic tests for Units I–VIII appear on pages 24–53 in this teacher's guide. To administer the diagnostic text for a unit, give each student a copy of the test; have students complete all sections independently; then collect the tests and check students' answers. Answers to these tests appear on pages 56–57 of this teacher's guide. Afterward, look at each student's errors. On the basis of the patterns you note, you may want to adjust instruction in one of these ways:

- If a small group of students show by their responses that they are not at all familiar with a skill, you may want to provide a pre-lesson tutorial on that skill for those students.

- If the majority of the class indicate through their responses that they are not at all familiar with a skill that will be taught in the unit, you may want to utilize one of the whole-class guided learning procedures outlined in "Adapting Lessons to Meet Students' Individual Needs" when presenting that lesson.

- If some students show by their responses that they are already familiar with a skill to be taught, you may want to have them either skip that lesson, complete it as homework, or serve as peer tutors for that lesson to students who need work on that skill.

Be sure to retain students' tests so you can compare their performance on each section with their performance on the same section of the achievement test, which is to be administered at the conclusion of the unit. Use the record-keeping form on page 60 of this teacher's guide to record test scores.

Achievement Tests. Each unit's achievement test checks students' progress with the unit skills and provides information that can be used to develop a plan for targeted remediation and additional practice. Reproducible masters of achievement tests for Units I–VIII appear on pages 26–55 in this teacher's guide. Administer the achievement test for a unit in the same manner as the diagnostic test. Answers for these tests appear on pages 58–59. Afterward, compare each student's performance on each section with his or her performance on the same section of the diagnostic test. Note areas of progress and areas in which remedial work is needed. For students needing remediation in a particular skill, it is recommended that you repeat the lesson that focuses on the problem area, and have them work through the exercises a second time using one of the procedures outlined in the section headed "Adapting Lessons for Students with Less Proficiency" in this teacher's guide.

You may want to record each student's performance on the individual student record-keeping form on page 60 of this teacher's guide.

Writing Assessment. Suggestions for assessing students' writing progress appear in the section entitled "Teaching Composition" on pages 17–20 of this teacher's guide. A rubric and checklists for evaluating writing lessons appear on pages 61–65.

INFORMAL ASSESSMENT IN *PRACTICAL GUIDE TO BETTER ENGLISH*

Observation/Holistic Assessment. Observing and making note of individual students' performance on various tasks during the course of each unit is an important part of the assessment process.

Among the many productive focuses for informal observation are the following:

- Students' performance on the exercises, including how much help they need to be able to complete the exercises.

- Students' knowledge of grammar, usage, and mechanics concepts as evidenced in their responses to questions asked of them.

- Students' willingness to try using new vocabulary and specialized terms in oral discussions.

- Students' use of correct and incorrect word forms in class discussions.

- Students' use of correct and incorrect word forms in written work for literature study, and in papers written for other classes.

- Students' attitude toward completing the exercises and writing tasks.

- Students' choice of books and magazines for independent reading.

Space for recording observations and anecdotal records of progress is provided on the individual student record-keeping form.

Student Self-Monitoring. Students can monitor themselves as they work through the unit by making note of what they do and do not understand, either in a personal journal or directly on the lesson pages. Encourage them also to use the practice items in the Handbook Guides as a quick method of assessing whether they understand a new rule or concept. The score chart that appears on page 176 of the student book provides a further means for students to keep track of personal progress.

UNIT I
Diagnostic Test, page 1

PART I   Write *yes* before each group of words that is a sentence. Write *no* before each group of words that is not a sentence.

_____   1.   Alaska is by far the largest state.

_____   2.   The longest coastline of any state.

_____   3.   Mount McKinley's towering peaks.

_____   4.   Alaska's state flag shows the Big Dipper.

PART II   Place the appropriate end mark at the end of each sentence. If the sentence is a statement, write *S* in the blank before it. If it is a question, write *Q*. If it is an exclamation, write *E*.

_____   5.   When did Alaska become a state__

_____   6.   Alaska became the 49th state in 1959__

_____   7.   How cold is it in Sitka__

_____   8.   How beautiful the Northern Lights are__

PART III   Draw a line under each uncapitalized word that should begin with a capital letter.

9.   my cousin's name is arthur.

10.   his hometown is anchorage.

11.   my friend liam lives in juneau.

12.   alaska's biggest cities are anchorage, fairbanks, and juneau.

13.   the united states bought alaska from russia in 1867.

14.   at that time william h. seward was Secretary of State.

PART IV   Place commas where they are needed in the following sentences.

15.   Alaska is rich in oil timber and fish.

16.   Have you ever been to Kodiak Arthur?

17.   Yes Kodiak is an island in the Gulf of Alaska.

PRACTICAL GUIDE TO BETTER ENGLISH

PART V   Draw a line under the word that completes each sentence correctly.

18.   Alaskan winters (is, are) very cold.

19.   The lowest recorded temperature (is, are) 80 degrees below zero.

20.   It (was, were) recorded in 1971.

PART VI   Rewrite the following words. Use abbreviations wherever you can.

21.   Mister Jack London   _____

22.   Thursday, February 14   _____

23.   2266 Kodiak Street   _____

PART VII   Place necessary commas and end marks where they belong in these sentences.

24.   Arthur have you ever seen a whale

25.   Yes I've seen whales many times

26.   Killer whales are huge graceful and powerful

PART VIII   Find the four sentences in the following paragraph. Put the correct punctuation at the end of each sentence. Draw a line under each word that begins a sentence and so should be capitalized.

27—30.

jack London was a famous American writer known for his tales of the Alaskan frontier in his youth, London was a restless adventurer he worked in many different jobs, including ranch hand, sailor, and gold miner many of his books describe the rough, colorful life in mining camps and seaports

PRACTICAL GUIDE TO BETTER ENGLISH

UNIT I
Achievement Test, page 1

PART I Write *yes* before each group of words that is a sentence. Write *no* before each group of words that is not a sentence.

_____ 1.   The largest country in South America.

_____ 2.   Portuguese is Brazil's official language.

_____ 3.   The capital, Brasília, is 600 miles from the coast.

_____ 4.   About 75 percent of Brazil's population.

PART II Place the appropriate end mark at the end of each sentence. If the sentence is a statement, write *S* in the blank before it. If it is a question, write *Q*. If it is an exclamation, write *E*.

_____ 5.   When did Brazil declare its independence from Portugal__

_____ 6.   Brazil became a republic in 1889__

_____ 7.   How beautiful the Brazilian flag is__

_____ 8.   What does each color symbolize__

PART III Draw a line under each uncapitalized word that should begin with a capital letter.

9.   my cousins moved to texas.

10.   at first ricky and anna lived in austin.

11.   now they live in houston, near aunt lydia.

12.   those cities were named after stephen f. austin and sam houston.

13.   texas became one of the united states in 1845.

14.   texas is more than 220 times the size of rhode island.

PART IV Place commas where they are needed in the following sentences.

15.   Have you ever visited San Antonio Aunt Lydia?

16.   Yes I took a tour of the Alamo.

17.   Texas has been claimed by Spain France and Mexico at different times.

PRACTICAL GUIDE TO BETTER ENGLISH

PART V Draw a line under the word that completes each sentence correctly.

18. We (was, were) reading about the Texas economy.

19. Cattle, cotton, and petroleum (is, are) produced in Texas.

20. Today there (is, are) more workers in sales jobs than in the oil industry.

PART VI Rewrite the following words. Use abbreviations wherever you can.

21. Monday, August 29 _____

22. 555 Alamo Avenue _____

23. Mister Sam Houston _____

PART VII Place necessary commas and end marks where they belong in these sentences.

24. Aunt Lydia have you ever heard of River Walk

25. Yes it is in downtown San Antonio

26. It's a shady pleasant place to shop eat and stroll along the river

PART VIII Find the four sentences in the following paragraph. Put the correct punctuation at the end of each sentence. Draw a line under each word that begins a sentence and so should be capitalized.

27—30.

    texan Lyndon B. Johnson was Vice President on November 22, 1963, when President John F. Kennedy was assassinated on that tragic day, Johnson took the oath of office and became President before becoming Vice President, Johnson had been a leader in Congress his contacts there helped him get important legislation passed during his time as President

PRACTICAL GUIDE TO BETTER ENGLISH

UNIT II
Diagnostic Test, page 1

PART I Read the paragraph below and answer the questions.

    Few land mammals are as impressive as the grizzly bear. A male grizzly can weigh up to 500 pounds and stand more than eight feet tall. Though grizzlies have great strength, they are somewhat shy. They eat mostly fish and berries, and rarely attack unless provoked.

1.   What is the topic of this paragraph? _____

2.   What does the paragraph tell about the topic? _____

_____

_____

PART II Think about how a paragraph is written, using the paragraph above to help you. Then follow the directions below.

3.   Write a sentence that might begin a paragraph about cats.

_____

_____

4.   Now give three details you might include in the rest of the paragraph.

A. _____

B. _____

C. _____

PART III Place quotation marks and commas where they are needed in these sentences.

5.   Have you ever seen a grizzly bear? I asked my Uncle Zeke.

6.   He replied I saw plenty of grizzlies in Wyoming.

7.   I asked Are there are many grizzlies in Wyoming?

8.   He said There are about 200 grizzly bears in Yellowstone National Park.

PART IV Punctuate the following direct and indirect quotations, adding necessary quotation marks, commas, and other punctuation.

9.   Uncle Zeke explained that bears are usually shy

10. Female bears protect their young fiercely he said

11. Never approach a bear cub he cautioned

12. I told him that I'd remember his advice

PRACTICAL GUIDE TO BETTER ENGLISH

PART V Draw a line under the word that completes each sentence correctly.

13. I asked Uncle Zeke if he would (teach, learn) me about wildlife photography.

14. He said, "You (can, may) learn if you are patient."

15. I've already been (taught, learned) to develop film.

16. (May, Can) I take a look at that photograph?

PART VI Write a contraction for each pair of words.

17. have not _____   19. will not _____

18. were not _____   20. could not _____

PART VII Draw a line under the appropriate words in parentheses. At the end of each sentence, write the contraction of the words you have underlined.

21. I (has not, have not) found my camera. _____

22. We (was not, were not) home yesterday. _____

PART VIII Correct the use of double negatives in these sentences by rewriting each one.

23. Uncle Zeke didn't see no grizzlies on his last trip.

_____

24. The bears wouldn't have nothing to do with him.

_____

25. I didn't have no film left.

_____

PART IX Draw a line under the word that correctly completes each sentence.

26. We had (driven, drove) high into the Rocky Mountains.

27. We (gone, went) to Wyoming on a photo expedition.

28. We (saw, seen) elk, deer, and foxes.

29. Uncle Zeke has (gone, went) on some unsuccessful photo shoots.

30. I (know, known) that wild animals don't always cooperate with photographers.

UNIT II
Achievement Test, page 1

PART I   Read the paragraph below and answer the questions.

The avocado is a fruit, not a vegetable. Each fruit has yellow-green pulp and contains one large seed. People eat avocados in salads, dips, and even desserts. Guacamole, a popular Mexican dish, is made from mashed avocados, tomatoes, onions, garlic, cilantro, and salt.

1.   What is the topic of this paragraph?   _____

2.   What does the paragraph tell about the topic? _____

_____

_____

PART II   Think about how a paragraph is written, using the paragraph above to help you. Then follow the directions below.

3.   Write a sentence that might begin a paragraph about corn.

_____

_____

4.   Now give three details you might include in the rest of the paragraph.

A. _____

B. _____

C. _____

PART III   Place quotation marks and commas where they are needed in these sentences.

5.   Is a tomato a fruit or a vegetable? Romy asked.

6.   I replied I'm fairly sure it is a fruit.

7.   Romy asked Then why don't people eat tomatoes for dessert?

8.   Not all fruits taste good as desserts Alvin said.

PART IV   Punctuate the following direct and indirect quotations, adding necessary quotation marks, commas, and other punctuation.

9.   He explained that some vegetables are used as dessert ingredients

10.   Do you remember the carrot cake Rudolph made I asked

11.   Romy recalled that some pies are not sweet

12.   Chicken pie and broccoli quiche are two examples she said

PRACTICAL GUIDE TO BETTER ENGLISH

Unit II Achievement Test, page 2

PART V Draw a line under the word that completes each sentence correctly.

13. Now that I am living alone, I need to (teach, learn) how to make some simple dishes.

14. Will you (teach, learn) me how to bake a quiche?

15 Anyone (may, can) learn how to make the filling.

16. (Can, May) I help you make the pie crust, too?

PART VI Write a contraction for each pair of words.

17. would not _____   19. did not _____

18. does not _____   20. are not _____

PART VII Draw a line under the appropriate words in parentheses. At the end of each sentence, write the contraction of the words you have underlined.

21. Dad (has not, have not) come back from the store yet. _____

22. I (has not, have not) finished chopping the onions. _____

PART VIII Correct the use of double negatives in these sentences by rewriting each one.

23. I don't put no cream in my quiche.

_____

24. She says there isn't nothing wrong with using milk.

_____

25. We don't have no cream, anyway.

_____

PART IX Draw a line under the word that correctly completes each sentence.

26. Dad (gone, went) to buy a frozen pie shell.

27. He (driven, drove) to the store after lunch.

28. Dad has (wrote, written) the recipe on this card.

29. I (knew, known) that quiches have eggs in them.

30. I've always (know, known) that I would make a good chef.

PRACTICAL GUIDE TO BETTER ENGLISH

UNIT III
Diagnostic Test, page 1

PART I   Use the following information to write a friendly letter. Write your letter on the lines below. Put the five parts of the letter where they belong.

1–4.

Dear Dean How's life in Boston? I heard you made the varsity baseball team. Let me know how your season is going. Your friend Dwight May 10, 1999

_____

_____

_____

_____

_____

_____

_____

PART II   Address this envelope to Mister Samuel Parker, 2266 Broadway Boulevard, Lansing, Michigan 48924. Place your own return address in the upper left-hand corner. Use abbreviations wherever they are appropriate.

5–8.

```



```

PART III   Rewrite the following sentences, adding capital letters and punctuation marks where they belong.

9.   last Saturday the seattle mariners played the cleveland indians

_____

10. did you see jay buhner play i asked leon

_____

11. yes he hit three home runs leon replied

_____

12. i said that I like watching randy johnson pitch

_____

PART IV Draw a line under each noun in these sentences.

13–14. Baseball is popular across the country.

15–16. Fans cheer for their favorite teams.

PART V Write the plural form of each noun below.

17. bush _____   19. fly _____

18. child _____   20. shelf _____

PART VI In the blank, write the possessive form of each word in parentheses.

21. (Astros) the _____ new pitcher

22. (children) the _____ favorite player

23. (boy) the _____ mitt

PART VII Decide which boldfaced word is the subject of each sentence. Draw a line under that word.

24. The **bases** were **loaded.**

25. **Karla** was **up** at bat.

26. The **pitcher** glared at **her.**

27. The **pitch** was **low** and outside.

PART VIII Rewrite the following sentences, adding correct punctuation.

28. The next batters appearance drew cheers from the crowd.

_____

29. Hit one out of the park a spectator yelled

_____

30. The players uniforms were green blue and white

_____

PRACTICAL GUIDE TO BETTER ENGLISH

UNIT III
Achievement Test, page 1

PART I Use the following information to write a friendly letter. Write your letter on the lines below. Put the five parts of the letter where they belong.

1–4.

Dear Danny I'm planning to visit my uncle in Los Angeles this summer. Will you be in town during the first two weeks in August? Let's get together! Your friend James April 2, 1999

_____

_____

_____

_____

_____

_____

PART II Address this envelope to Mister James Kwan, 12121 Pine Street, Beverly, Massachusetts 01915. Place your own return address in the upper left-hand corner. Use abbreviations whenever they are appropriate.

5–8.

```



```

PART III Rewrite the following sentences, adding capital letters and punctuation marks where they belong.

9. james and danny went to santa monica beach last weekend

_____

10. do you ever see any movie stars here in los angeles asked james

   _____

11. no most of the movie stars live in malibu or pacific palisades danny said

   _____

12. once i saw sean penn in a coffee shop he added

   _____

PART IV Draw a line under each noun in these sentences.

13–14. We can rent bikes at the beach.

15–16. This store sells huge sandwiches.

PART V Write the plural form of each noun below.

17. man _____ 19. wolf _____

18. dairy _____ 20. beach _____

PART VI In the blank, write the possessive form of each word in parentheses.

21. (Danny) _____ videotapes

22. (women) _____ favorite movies

23. (movie stars) _____ homes

PART VII Decide which boldfaced word is the subject of each sentence. Draw a line under that word.

24. The **temperature** was in the **nineties.**

25. **Danny** had **forgotten** his sunscreen.

26. That **store** sells **sunscreen.**

27. **James** has some **in** his backpack.

PART VIII Rewrite the following sentences, adding correct punctuation.

28. There's something on your towel yelled Danny

   _____

29. A small nervous crab scuttled off Ricks towel

   _____

30. That little crabs shell had red beige and white markings

   _____

PRACTICAL GUIDE TO BETTER ENGLISH

UNIT IV
Diagnostic Test, page 1

PART I Draw a line under each noun in the sentences below.

1. Robins live throughout the continent.

2. Rachel saw several robins on her lawn.

In these sentences, pronouns have been substituted for some of the nouns in the sentences above. Underline each pronoun.

3. They live throughout the continent.

4. She saw several robins on it.

PART II Draw a line under the pronoun that completes each sentence correctly.

5. (Us, We) went on a hike last week.

6. Darius and (I, me) saw a bee hummingbird.

7. (It, They) was just two inches tall.

8. (They, Them) build nests the size of walnuts.

PART III Draw a line under the pronoun that completes each sentence correctly.

9. The hummingbird ignored Teresa and (I, me) completely.

10. My brother handed (she, her) his binoculars.

11. Darius gave (I, me) a field guide to birds.

12. We also got some birdwatching tips from (he, him).

PART IV Draw a line under the word or phrase that correctly completes each sentence.

13. My brother asked (Darius and I, Darius and me) for help.

14. It was (I, me) who agreed.

15. My brother showed (him and me, he and I) a picture of a kingfisher.

16. (Me and Darius, Darius and I) promised to look for one.

PART V   Substitute pronouns for the underlined nouns or noun groups.

17.   <u>Darius</u> and <u>Michelle</u> saw <u>a vulture</u>.

_____ and _____ saw _____.

18.   <u>Vultures</u> eat <u>dead animals</u>.

_____ eat _____.

19.   Now <u>Darius</u> is looking for <u>a hawk</u>.

Now _____ is looking for _____.

PART VI   Draw a line through each unnecessary word in the sentences below.

20.   These here binoculars are very useful.

21.   My brother he never goes bird watching without them.

22.   Darius went and borrowed the binoculars without asking.

23.   My brother asked, "Where are you going to, Darius?"

PART VII   Read this paragraph. Cross out the two sentences that do not belong there.

24–25.

The osprey is a powerful bird of prey. Ospreys nest in the tops of tall trees. Their distinctive black and white markings make them easy to identify. Many beautiful birds are on display at the zoo. Ospreys are excellent fishers. These birds hover in the air, watching the water with their sharp eyes. Ospreys dive straight into the water to catch fish. The American dipper can walk underwater! Ospreys grasp the wriggling fish with their sharp talons.

PART VIII   Rewrite this paragraph on the lines, changing some of the nouns to pronouns.

26–28.

The robin returned to the robin's nest. Rachel asked Darius for the binoculars, and Darius gave them to Rachel. Darius and Rachel watched the baby robins welcome the baby robins' mother.

_____

_____

_____

_____

PART IX   Underline each word that should begin with a capital letter and add necessary punctuation.

29.   john james audubon painted the birds of north america

30.   didn't audubon study birds in america scotland and england

PRACTICAL GUIDE TO BETTER ENGLISH

UNIT IV
Achievement Test, page 1

PART I Draw a line under each noun in the sentences below.

1. Dogs have lived with humans for 10,000 years.

2. Skipper helps her master herd sheep.

In these sentences, pronouns have been substituted for some of the nouns in the sentences above. Underline each pronoun.

3. They have lived with us for 10,000 years.

4. She helps him herd sheep.

PART II Draw a line under the pronoun that completes each sentence correctly.

5. Aaron and (I, me) visited the Smithfield Guide Dog Center.

6. (He, Him) and I went to see some golden retriever pups.

7. (They, Them) leaped and yelped excitedly.

8. (Us, We) met Jessica outside.

PART III Draw a line under the pronoun that completes each sentence correctly.

9. The mother dog trusted Aaron and (I, me).

10. She let (he, him) and me pet the puppies.

11. Mr. Fresco smiled at (us, we) and told us the mother dog's name.

12. Maude is a perfect name for (she, her).

PART IV Draw a line under the word or phrase that correctly completes each sentence.

13. Mr. Fresco explained the training process to (Jessica and I, Jessica and me).

14. It is (he, him) who trains most of the dogs at the Center.

15. He showed (she and I, her and me) how a dog guides its owner.

16. (Me and Jessica, Jessica and I) were amazed at the dogs' intelligence.

PRACTICAL GUIDE TO BETTER ENGLISH

PART V Substitute pronouns for the underlined nouns or noun groups.

17. Jessica bought a dog-training book.

   _____ bought _____.

18. The puppies wagged their tails.

   _____ wagged _____.

19. Now Maude is wagging her tail at Aaron.

   Now _____ is wagging her tail at _____.

PART VI Draw a line through each unnecessary word in the sentences below.

20. This here Labrador retriever has a shiny black coat.

21. She knows like twenty different commands.

22. Mr. Fresco he let us buckle Max's harness.

23. "Where are you and Max going to?" I asked.

PART VII Read this paragraph. Cross out the three sentences that do not belong there.

24–25.

    Hearing-ear dogs are trained to call hearing-impaired people's attention to important sounds, such as ringing telephones and crying babies. Babies cry when they are hungry. The first national training program for hearing dogs started in 1976. The Humane Society and several other organizations run these programs today. Australian shepherds help humans herd sheep and cattle. A hearing dog can also alert its owner to alarm clocks, doorbells, and smoke alarms. Most pet dogs are loyal and friendly.

PART VIII Rewrite this paragraph on the lines, changing some of the nouns to pronouns.

26–28.

    Jenny and Max are Maude's pups. They have silky ears, cold noses, and feet that are too big for Jenny and Max. Maude feeds her pups and keeps her pups clean. Sometimes Jenny and Max seem to get on Maude's nerves, however. Then Maude barks at Jenny and Max.

_____

_____

_____

_____

PART IX Underline each word that should begin with a capital letter and add necessary punctuation.

29. famous cartoon dogs include goofy snoopy and odie

30. charlotte asked isn't snoopy a character created by charles schulz

PRACTICAL GUIDE TO BETTER ENGLISH

UNIT V
Diagnostic Test, page 1

PART I Rewrite the names below, using the correct title before each name. If the title can be abbreviated, use the abbreviation.

1. Rasheed Magalin (a dentist)   _____

2. Darla Benedict (a married woman)   _____

3. Kimberly Wong (a senator)   _____

4. Randolph B. Comisky (a man)   _____

5. Kelly Matsumoto (an unmarried woman)   _____

PART II Answer the advertisement below by writing a business letter to the manager of Outdoor Supplies Unlimited. Include all the parts of a business letter and arrange them properly. Use your own address as the heading in the upper right-hand corner. Write your letter on the lines below.

6–10. For a free catalog of our camping products, write to Outdoor Suppliers Unlimited, 4400 Peak Road, Boulder, Colorado 80301.

_____

_____

_____

_____

_____

_____

_____   _____

_____

_____

_____

_____

PART III Read each word to yourself. If the first syllable has a long vowel sound, write *long* on the line. If the first syllable has a short vowel sound, write *short* on the line.

11. silent   _____

12. melon   _____

PRACTICAL GUIDE TO BETTER ENGLISH

PART IV   Write each word. Draw a line between the syllables. Use the example above each column to help you.

po-ny   rob-in

13.   paper   _____   15.   medal   _____

14.   moment   _____   16.   lemon   _____

PART V   Underline the word that correctly completes each sentence.

17.   (Whose, Who's) canteen is this?

18.   Put your knapsack over (hear, here).

19.   I don't (no, know) where my compass is.

20.   (It's, Its) right in your pocket.

PART VI   Underline the word that correctly completes each sentence.

21.   Look at the litter (lying, lain) on the ground.

22.   Ana will (laid, lay) her pack against that rock.

23.   Don't (lay, lays) your blanket on an anthill.

PART VII   In each blank, write the verb *lie* or the verb *lay*.

24.   We should _____ down and rest awhile.

25.   You can _____ your pack down there.

26.   Dave will _____ a tarp down.

27.   I'll _____ in the shade of this tree.

PART VIII   Underline each word that should begin with a capital letter and add other necessary punctuation marks.

28.   do you know anton spitzer from tacoma washington luis asked

29.   yes anton is a friend from the university of washington madeline replied

30.   in june 1998 anton and i visited carlsbad caverns in new mexico she continued

PRACTICAL GUIDE TO BETTER ENGLISH

Name_____ Date _____

UNIT V
Achievement Test, *page 1*

PART I   Rewrite the names below, using the correct title before each name. If the title can be abbreviated, use the abbreviation.

1.   Linda Elder (a married woman)   _____

2.   Daniel Pine (a man)   _____

3.   Frank Ortiz (a doctor)   _____

4.   Andrew Kirsch (a governor)   _____

5.   Sophie Kamin (an unmarried woman)   _____

PART II   Answer the advertisement below by writing a business letter to The Golden Paintbrush. Include all the parts of a business letter and arrange them properly. Use your own address as the heading in the upper right-hand corner. Write your letter on the lines below.

6–10.   For a free catalog of our art supplies, write to The Golden Paintbrush, 5665 Mesquite Boulevard, San Antonio, Texas 78212.

_____

_____

_____

_____

_____

_____

_____

_____

_____

_____

_____

PART III   Read each word to yourself. If the first syllable has a long vowel sound, write *long* on the line. If the first syllable has a short vowel sound, write *short* on the line.

11.   petal   _____

12.   local   _____

PRACTICAL GUIDE TO BETTER ENGLISH

PART IV Write each word. Draw a line between the syllables. Use the example above each column to help you.

mi-nus   min-ute

13. label _____   15. model _____

14. yogurt _____   16. timid _____

PART V Underline the word that correctly completes each sentence.

17. Have you ever (one, won) a contest?

18. I (no, know) someone who received first prize in a July 4th recipe contest.

19. He created a red, white, and (blew, blue) fruit sundae.

20. (Its, It's) ingredients were strawberries, blueberries, and yogurt.

PART VI Underline the word that correctly completes each sentence.

21. Please (lay, lie) the cookbook here on the counter.

22. I (laid, lays) the lettuce on a towel to dry.

23. Our dog is (lying, lain) on the kitchen floor.

PART VII In each blank, write the verb *lie* or the verb *lay*.

24. I'm going to _____ on the couch.

25. Please _____ a blanket over my legs.

26. You should _____ your sweater on the counter.

27. Otherwise the cat will _____ on it.

PART VIII Underline each word that should begin with a capital letter and add other necessary punctuation marks.

28. can you cook any asian dishes trish asked

29. yes i learned to cook in beijing china Kam Yung replied

30. our family moved to los angeles california in september 1992 she continued

PRACTICAL GUIDE TO BETTER ENGLISH

UNIT VI
Diagnostic Test, page 1

PART I Draw a line under the verb that correctly completes each sentence.

1. That honey (came, come) from orange blossoms.

2. It (was, were) collected by hundreds of worker bees.

3. The bees have (flew, flown) great distances.

4. They (is, are) energetic workers.

PART II Draw a line under the pronoun that correctly completes each sentence.

5. (We, us) beekeepers must be cautious.

6. You and (I, me) can visit the hive.

7. You can help (I, me) collect honey.

PART III Place apostrophes where they belong in these sentences.

8. This bees job is guarding the hive.

9. Some bees dont collect nectar.

10. The queens job is laying eggs.

11. She doesnt have to do any work.

PART IV Draw a line under the word that correctly completes each sentence.

12. Look at those bees to (your, you're) left.

13. (Their, They're) collecting pollen.

14. They store the pollen in a sack on (there, their) legs.

15. (Your, You're) distracting the bees with that radio!

PART V Write the possessive form of each pronoun in parentheses.

16. (I) _____ dad taught me to tend bees.

17. (He) _____ favorite honey is wildflower honey.

18. (it) A bee that has lost _____ stinger may die.

19. (They) Bees will risk _____ lives for the hive's welfare.

PRACTICAL GUIDE TO BETTER ENGLISH

PART VI Draw a line under the word that best completes each new sentence.

20. What are (them, those) bees doing?

21. Beekeepers must protect (themselves, himself).

22. Are (them, those) gloves yours?

PART VII Draw a line under the word that best completes each sentence.

23. Please (sit, set) the honey on the table.

24. (Sit, Set) down and I'll let you taste it.

25. You're (setting, sitting) on the lid!

PART VIII Rewrite the sentences below so they give a clearer picture of what is being described. Add details to each sentence.

26. A girl picked a flower from a bush.

_____

_____

27. She heard a sound coming from the flower.

_____

_____

28. When a bee flew out, she dropped the flower and ran.

_____

_____

PART IX Underline each word that should begin with a capital letter, and add necessary punctuation.

29. kathy will you finish your report about bees by friday mario asked

30. yes it will be the greatest insect study ever done at roosevelt high replied kathy

PRACTICAL GUIDE TO BETTER ENGLISH

UNIT VI
Achievement Test, page 1

PART I Draw a line under the verb that correctly completes each sentence.

1. The scientists (flew, flown) to South America last year.

2. They (gone, went) there to study tarantulas.

3. It (was, were) a successful expedition.

4. They have (become, became) experts on tarantulas.

PART II Draw a line under the pronoun that correctly completes each sentence.

5. (We, Us) students are learning about spiders' eating habits.

6. Mrs. Wu told (I, me) that spiders can't eat solid food.

7. She told (we, us) that they "drink" their prey.

PART III Place apostrophes where they belong in these sentences.

8. That tarantulas fangs pump digestive fluid into a cockroach.

9. The huge spider cant eat the cockroach yet.

10. It must wait until the cockroachs body has liquefied.

11. Its table manners arent very attractive.

PART IV Draw a line under the word that correctly completes each sentence.

12. Is that (your, you're) magazine on the table?

13. I noticed that (your, you're) reading about tarantulas.

14. Tarantulas have pads on the bottoms of (there, their) feet.

15. (They're, There) like tiny air pillows.

PART V Write the possessive form of each pronoun in parentheses.

16. (I) _____ aunt studies tarantulas at the University of Arizona.

17. (She) _____ pet tarantula is named Tinkerbelle.

18. (it) A tarantula feels tiny vibrations through _____ body hairs.

19. (They) Tarantulas need this warning system because _____ vision is poor.

PRACTICAL GUIDE TO BETTER ENGLISH

PART VI Draw a line under the word that best completes each new sentence.

20. (Them, These) body hairs can be used as weapons, too.

21. Some tarantulas defend (itself, themselves) by shooting tiny barbed hairs into attackers.

22. (Them, Those) hairs can cause terrible itching for months.

PART VII Draw a line under the word that best completes each sentence.

23. Please (set, sit) my camera on that rock.

24. I'm going to (set, sit) here until a tarantula appears.

25. That tarantula is (setting, sitting) still, waiting for prey to approach.

PART VIII Rewrite the sentences below so they give a clearer picture of what is being described. Add details to each sentence.

26. A boy saw a spider on the ceiling.

   _____

   _____

27. He watched the spider spin a web.

   _____

   _____

28. He saw a fly land on it and try to get away.

   _____

   _____

PART IX Underline each word that should begin with a capital letter, and add necessary punctuation.

29. stacy asked did you make that drawing when you were in south america

30. dr stanley replied yes the spider I drew is named after a giant called goliath.

PRACTICAL GUIDE TO BETTER ENGLISH

UNIT VII
Diagnostic Test, page 1

PART I Arrange the following words in alphabetical order.

golf   brig   1. _____   4. _____

buck   artifact   2. _____   5. _____

bugle   mellow   3. _____   6. _____

PART II Use a dictionary to help you complete these items. First, circle the correctly spelled word in each pair. Then write that word on the line. Divide the word into syllables, and place an accent mark after the syllable that should be stressed.

7.   famly   family   _____

8.   business   buisness   _____

9.   usuly   usually   _____

10.   What kinds of information can you find in a dictionary? Circle the letters next to your answers.

A.   information about where a word comes from

B.   directions for how to write an essay

C.   information about how a word is pronounced, or said

D.   different meanings a word can have.

PART III Consult a dictionary to find the answers to these questions. Write your answers on the lines.

11.   How many feet are in a *rod*?   _____

12.   What kind of animal is a *hackney*?   _____

13.   Which word is pronounced like *heir—air* or *hair*?   _____

PART IV Choose a synonym for each word. Write the synonym on the line.

frighten   sudden   comfort

14.   abrupt   _____

15.   scare   _____

16.   soothe   _____

PRACTICAL GUIDE TO BETTER ENGLISH

PART V   Choose an antonym for each word. Write the antonym on the line.

enter   follow   guilty

17.   exit   _____

18.   innocent   _____

19.   lead   _____

PART VI   Draw a line under the word that correctly completes each sentence.

20.   Have you (read, red) any good books lately?

21.   I finished a great novel last (weak, week).

22.   It was about a sailor who was lost at (sea, see).

PART VII   Draw a line under each adjective in the sentences below. (Do not underline the articles *a*, *an*, and *the*.) Then draw a box around each adverb.

23.   The lost sailor rowed furiously.

24.   His tiny boat tossed violently in the waves.

PART VIII   Draw a line under the word that correctly completes each sentence.

25.   The sailor (was, were) caught in a typhoon.

26.   He was clinging to a life raft by (himself, hisself).

27.   (Don't, Doesn't) that sound scary?

PART IX   Underline each word that should begin with a capital letter, and add necessary punctuation.

28.   the sailors luck changed near puerto rico

29.   a fisher named juan morales plucked him out of the caribbean ocean on may 12 1999

30.   youre a very fortunate person juan said to the sailor

PRACTICAL GUIDE TO BETTER ENGLISH

UNIT VII
Achievement Test, page 1

PART I   Arrange the following words in alphabetical order.

umbrella   title   1. _____   4. _____

tricycle   melon   2. _____   5. _____

trampoline branch   3. _____   6. _____

PART II   Use a dictionary to help you complete these items. First, circle the correctly spelled word in each pair. Then write that word on the line. Divide the word into syllables, and place an accent mark after the syllable that should be stressed.

7.   coud   could   _____

8.   hundred   hunderd   _____

9.   receive   recieve   _____

10.   What kinds of information can you find in a dictionary? Circle the letters next to your answers.

   A.   directions for how to write a letter
   B.   information about how a word is pronounced, or said
   C.   different meanings a word can have
   D.   information about where a word comes from

PART III   Consult a dictionary to find the answers to these questions. Write your answers on the lines.

11.   In what part of the body is the *parietal* bone?   _____

12.   Does the word *clique* rhyme with *pick* or *peak*?   _____

13.   How many feet equal a *fathom*?   _____

PART IV   Choose a synonym for each word. Write the synonym on the line.

      rigid   rapid   enemy

14.   foe   _____

15.   swift   _____

16.   inflexible _____

PRACTICAL GUIDE TO BETTER ENGLISH

PART V   Choose an antonym for each word. Write the antonym on the line.

       filthy   selfish   bored

17.   fascinated   _____

18.   spotless   _____

19.   generous   _____

PART VI   Draw a line under the word that correctly completes each sentence.

20.   Will you (great, grate) some cheese for me?

21.   The pizza will be ready in (eight, ate) minutes.

22.   (Wood, Would) you like to stay for dinner?

PART VII   Draw a line under each adjective in the sentences below. (Do not underline the articles *a*, *an*, and *the*.) Then draw a box around each adverb.

23.   The thick pizza cooked slowly.

24.   Hungry guests impatiently waited for dinner.

PART VIII   Draw a line under the word that correctly completes each sentence.

25.   The guests (was, were) delighted with the pizza.

26.   Zack made the sauce (himself, hisself).

27.   (Weren't, Wasn't) the roasted peppers delicious?

PART IX   Underline each word that should begin with a capital letter, and add necessary punctuation.

28.   kelsie graduated from the academy of fine cuisine in new york city

29.   our friends graduation from cooking school was on june 26 1998

30.   shes going to make dinner for mateo and me said carmina

UNIT VIII
Diagnostic Test, *page 1*

PART I   Combine the short pairs of sentences into a longer sentence. Use the word *and* in your sentences. You may need to change other words, too.

Kenny plays the guitar. Angela plays the flute.

1.   _____

Kenny is very talented. Angela is very talented.

2.   _____

PART II   Combine the short sentences into one longer sentence. Use one of the words below to connect them.

but   because   although

Angela is a little worried. Kenny feels ill tonight.

3.   _____

Angela can perform solo. She prefers to play with other musicians.

4.   _____

PART III   Rewrite this paragraph on the lines below. Combine the short sentences into longer, better ones. Use connecting words such as *and, because,* and *but* to join the sentences.

5–7.   Kenny plays music at Mr. Lim's restaurant. Angela plays music at Mr. Lim's restaurant. Dinner hour is always packed. Customers love the music. Kenny is sick tonight. Angela will play anyway.

_____

_____

_____

PART IV   Draw a line under the contraction that correctly completes each sentence.

8.   (Doesn't, Don't) Angela play the saxophone, too?

9.   I (hasn't, haven't) seen Kenny's new guitar.

10.   The musicians (isn't, aren't) nervous at all.

11.   (Wasn't, Weren't) they practicing yesterday?

PRACTICAL GUIDE TO BETTER ENGLISH

PART V In each sentence, underline the verb or verb phrase once. Underline the direct object twice.

12. Celia plays the mandolin.

13. Kenny bought a new guitar.

14. They play music together.

15. Angela has written a very funny song.

PART VI Draw one line under the simple subject in each sentence. Draw two lines under the simple predicate. Circle each predicate noun or predicate adjective. On the line, write whether the word you circled is a predicate noun or a predicate adjective.

16. My guitar is old. _____

17. The harp is a beautiful instrument. _____

18. The musicians are nervous. _____

PART VII Draw a line under the word or phrase that correctly completes each sentence.

19. I (heered, heard) some new CDs last night.

20. I (might not have, might not of) discovered them at all.

21. Kenny (has, has got) great taste in music.

22. We (must have, must of) listened to five CDs.

23. I'd never heard (none, any) of B. B. King's music before.

PART VIII Draw a line under the word that correctly completes each sentence.

24. That CD is (our's, ours).

25. Celia and I (gone, went) downtown to buy it.

26. Have you (saw, seen) Rockin' Rudy's record store?

27. (Isn't, Aren't) their selection the best in town?

PART IX Underline each word that should begin with a capital letter, and add necessary punctuation marks.

28. whos john lee hooker i asked mr martin

29. hes one of americas greatest blues guitar players he answered

30. he has performed with bonnie raitt john hiatt and van morrison, just to name a few he continued

PRACTICAL GUIDE TO BETTER ENGLISH

UNIT VIII
Achievement Test, page 1

PART I Combine the short pairs of sentences into a longer sentence. Use the word *and* in your sentences. You may need to change other words, too.

Stan paints pictures. Laura takes photographs.

1. _____

Stan is very successful. Laura is very successful.

2. _____

PART II Combine the short sentences into one longer sentence. Use one of the words below to connect them.

because   but   until

Stan is happy for Laura. She won first prize in the city arts contest.

3. _____

_____

Laura cannot collect the prize money. She goes to City Hall.

4. _____

_____

PART III Rewrite this paragraph on the lines below. Combine the short sentences into longer, better ones. Use connecting words such as *and, because,* and *but* to join the sentences.

5–7.   Stan goes to art galleries. Laura goes to art galleries. They like to look at other artists' work. It inspires them. Stan is busy this afternoon. Laura will go anyway.

_____

_____

_____

PART IV Draw a line under the contraction that correctly completes each sentence.

8.   (Doesn't, Don't) Stan draw cartoons, too?

9.   I (hasn't, haven't) seen his newest comic strip.

10.   Stan and Laura (isn't, aren't) going to the art show.

11.   (Wasn't, Weren't) Stan the winner of last year's contest?

PRACTICAL GUIDE TO BETTER ENGLISH

PART V In each sentence, underline the verb or verb phrase once. Underline the direct object twice.

12. Stan paints portraits.

13. Sara bought some paintbrushes.

14. Ann makes beautiful weavings.

15. Ophelia has sold a large painting.

PART VI Draw one line under the simple subject in each sentence. Draw two lines under the simple predicate. Circle each predicate noun or predicate adjective. On the line, write whether the word you circled is a predicate noun or a predicate adjective.

16. That painting is colorful. _____

17. Stan is the artist. _____

18. The brushstrokes are dramatic. _____

PART VII Draw a line under the word or phrase that correctly completes each sentence.

19. You (should have, should of) seen the art show in the park.

20. There (must of, must have) been a hundred artists there.

21. Our city (has got, has) an excellent arts council.

22. I (might not of, might not have) become an artist without their support.

23. I (heard, heered) they created a program called Art on Wheels.

PART VIII Draw a line under the word that correctly completes each sentence.

24. I finally (seen, saw) Stan's new portrait of Laura.

25. (Isn't, Aren't) it painted with watercolors?

26. Bert and Josie (went, gone) downtown to see it.

27. (Don't, Doesn't) Stan use oil paints sometimes?

PART IX Underline each word that should begin with a capital letter, and add necessary punctuation marks.

28. have you ever seen georgia O'Keeffes famous flower paintings asked amy

29. her work was first displayed in new york city, and she became one of america's best-known artists said richard

30. she lived in many states, including wisconsin new york south carolina texas and new mexico he continued

PRACTICAL GUIDE TO BETTER ENGLISH

Answer Keys—Diagnostic Tests

UNIT I

1. yes
2. no
3. no
4. yes
5. Q ?
6. S .
7. Q ?
8. E !

9. <u>my</u> cousin's name is <u>arthur</u>.
10. <u>his</u> hometown is <u>anchorage</u>.
11. <u>my</u> friend <u>liam</u> lives in <u>juneau</u>.
12. <u>alaska's</u> biggest cities are <u>anchorage</u>, <u>fairbanks</u>, and <u>juneau</u>.
13. <u>the united states</u> bought <u>alaska</u> from <u>russia</u> in 1867.
14. <u>at that time</u> <u>william h. seward</u> was Secretary of State.
15. Alaska is rich in oil, timber, and fish.
16. Have you ever been to Kodiak, Arthur?
17. Yes, Kodiak is an island in the Gulf of Alaska.

18. are
19. is
20. was
21. Mr. Jack London
22. Thurs., Feb. 14
23. 2266 Kodiak St.

24. Arthur, have you ever seen a whale?
25. Yes, I've seen whales many times.
26. Killer whales are huge, graceful, and powerful.
27–30.

    Jack London was a famous American writer known for his tales of the Alaskan frontier. <u>in</u> his youth, London was a restless adventurer. <u>he</u> worked in many different jobs, including ranch hand, sailor, and gold miner. <u>many</u> of his books describe the rough, colorful life in mining camps and seaports.

UNIT II

Answers may vary for items 1–2.
1. grizzly bears
2. how heavy, tall, and strong grizzly bears are, how they behave, and what they eat

Answers will vary for items 3–4.
5. "Have you ever seen a grizzly bear?" I asked my Uncle Zeke.
6. He replied, "I saw plenty of grizzlies in Wyoming."
7. I asked, "Are there are many grizzlies in Wyoming?"
8. He said, "There are about 200 grizzly bears in Yellowstone National Park."
9. Uncle Zeke explained that bears are usually shy.
10. "Female bears protect their young fiercely," he said.
11. "Never approach a bear cub," he cautioned.
12. I told him that I'd remember his advice.

13. teach
14. can
15. taught
16. May
17. haven't
18. weren't
19. won't
20. couldn't

21. have not, haven't
22. were not, weren't

Answers may vary for items 23–25.
23. Uncle Zeke didn't see any grizzlies on his last trip.
24. The bears wouldn't have anything to do with him.
25. I didn't have any film left.

26. driven
27. went
28. saw
29. gone
30. know

UNIT III

1–4.

                      May 10, 1999

Dear Dean,
    How's life in Boston? I heard you made the varsity basketball team. Let me know how your season is going.

                  Your friend,
                  Dwight

5–8. <Student's address should be at upper left.>

    Mr. Samuel Parker
    2266 Broadway Blvd.
    Lansing, MI 48924

9. Last Saturday the Seattle Mariners played the Cleveland Indians.
10. "Did you see Jay Buhner play?" I asked Leon.
11. "Yes, he hit three home runs," Leon replied.
12. I said that I like watching Randy Johnson pitch.
13–14. Baseball is popular across the <u>country</u>.
15–16. <u>Fans</u> cheer for their favorite <u>teams</u>.

17. bushes
18. children
19. flies
20. shelves
21. Astros'
22. children's
23. boy's
24. bases
25. Karla
26. pitcher
27. pitch

28. The next batter's appearance drew cheers from the crowd.
29. "Hit one out of the park!" a spectator yelled.
30. The players' uniforms were green, blue, and white.

UNIT IV

1. Robins, continent
2. Rachel, robins, lawn
3. They
4. She, it
5. We
6. I
7. It
8. They
9. me
10. her
11. me
12. him
13. Darius and me
14. I
15. him and me
16. Darius and I
17. He and she saw it.
18. They eat them.
19. Now he is looking for it.
20. here
21. he
22. went, and
23. to

24–25. Many beautiful birds are on display at the zoo. The American dipper can walk underwater!
26–28. Answers may vary.
    The robin returned to its nest. Rachel asked Darius for the binoculars, and he gave them to her. They watched the baby robins welcome their mother.

29. john james audubon painted the birds of north america.
30. didn't audubon study birds in america, scotland, and england?

UNIT V

1. Dr. Rasheed Magalin
2. Mrs. Darla Benedict
3. Sen. Kimberly Wong
4. Mr. Randolph B. Comisky
5. Ms. or Miss Kelly Matsumoto

6–10. Answers may vary.

<student's address>
<today's date>

Manager
Outdoor Supplies Unlimited
4400 Peak Rd.
Boulder, CO 80301

Dear Manager:

Please send me a free catalog of your camping products. Thanks for your help.

Sincerely,
<student's signature>

11. long	17. Whose	23. lay
12. short	18. here	24. lie
13. pa-per	19. know	25. lay
14. mo-ment	20. It's	26. lay
15. med-al	21. lying	27. lie
16. lem-on	22. lay	

28. "do you know anton spitzer from tacoma, washington?" luis asked.
29. "yes, anton is a friend from the university of washington," madeline replied.
30. "in june 1998, anton and i visited carlsbad caverns in new mexico," she continued.

UNIT VI

1. came	10. queen's	19. their
2. was	11. doesn't	20. those
3. flown	12. your	21. themselves
4. are	13. They're	22. those
5. We	14. their	23. set
6. I	15. You're	24. Sit
7. me	16. My	25. sitting
8. bee's	17. His	
9. don't	18. its	

Answers will vary for items 26–28.

29. "kathy, will you finish your report about bees by friday?" mario asked.
30. "yes, it will be the greatest insect study ever done at roosevelt high," replied kathy.

UNIT VII

1. artifact	3. buck	5. golf
2. brig	4. bugle	6. mellow

7. family   fam´i-ly
8. business   busi´ness
9. usually   u´su-al-ly

10. A, C, D	15. frighten	20. read
11. 6 1/2	16. comfort	21. week
12. a horse	17. enter	22. sea
13. *air*	18. guilty	
14. sudden	19. follow	

23. The lost sailor rowed furiously .
24. His tiny boat tossed violently in the waves.
25. was
26. himself
27. Doesn't
28. the sailor's luck changed near puerto rico.
29. a fisher named juan morales plucked him out of the caribbean ocean on may 12, 1999.
30. "you're a very fortunate person," juan said to the sailor.

UNIT VIII

Answers for items 1–7 may vary.
1. Kenny plays the guitar, and Angela plays the flute.
2. Kenny and Angela are both very talented.
3. Angela is a little worried because Kenny feels ill tonight.
4. Although Angela can perform solo, she prefers to play with other musicians.
5–7. Kenny and Angela play music at Mr. Lim's restaurant. Dinner hour is always packed because customers love the music. Kenny is sick tonight, but Angela will play anyway.

8. Doesn't	10. aren't
9. haven't	11. Weren't

12. Celia plays the mandolin.
13. Kenny bought a new guitar.
14. They play music together.
15. Angela has written a very funny song.
16. My guitar is old. predicate adjective
17. The harp is a beautiful instrument. predicate noun
18. The musicians are nervous. predicate adjective

19. heard	22. must have	26. seen
20. might not have	23. any	27. Isn't
21. has	24. ours	
	25. went	

28. "who's john lee hooker?" i asked mr. martin.
29. "he's one of america's greatest blues guitar players," he answered.
30. "he has performed with bonnie raitt, john hiatt, and van morrison, just to name a few," he continued.

Answer Keys—Achievement Tests

UNIT I

1. no   3. yes   5. Q ?   7. E !
2. yes   4. no   6. S .   8. Q ?

9. <u>my</u> cousins moved to <u>texas</u>.
10. <u>at</u> first <u>ricky</u> and <u>anna</u> lived in <u>austin</u>.
11. <u>now</u> they live in <u>houston</u>, near <u>aunt lydia</u>.
12. <u>those</u> cities were named after <u>stephen f. austin</u> and <u>sam houston</u>.
13. <u>texas</u> became one of the <u>united states</u> in 1845.
14. <u>texas</u> is more than 220 times the size of <u>rhode island</u>.
15. Have you ever visited San Antonio, Aunt Lydia?
16. Yes, I took a tour of the Alamo.
17. Texas has been claimed by Spain, France, and Mexico at different times.

18. were   21. Mon., Aug. 29
19. are   22. 555 Alamo Ave.
20. are   23. Mr. Sam Houston

24. Aunt Lydia, have you ever heard of River Walk?
25. Yes, it is in downtown San Antonio.
26. It's a shady, pleasant place to shop, eat, and stroll along the river.

27–30.
   <u>texan</u> Lyndon B. Johnson was Vice President on November 22, 1963, when President John F. Kennedy was assassinated. <u>on</u> that tragic day, Johnson took the oath of office and became President. <u>before</u> becoming Vice President, Johnson had been a leader in Congress. <u>his</u> contacts there helped him get important legislation passed during his time as President.

UNIT II

Answers for items 1–2 may vary.

1. avocados
2. what they are, how they look, and what kinds of dishes they are used to make

Answers for items 3–4 will vary.

5. "Is a tomato a fruit or a vegetable?" Romy asked.
6. I replied, "I'm fairly sure it is a fruit."
7. Romy asked, "Then why don't people eat tomatoes for dessert?"
8. "Not all fruits taste good as desserts," Alvin said.
9. He explained that some vegetables are used as dessert ingredients.
10. "Do you remember the carrot cake Rudolph made?" I asked.
11. Romy recalled that some pies are not sweet.
12. "Chicken pie and broccoli quiche are two examples," she said.

13. learn   17. wouldn't   21. has not, hasn't
14. teach   18. doesn't
15. can   19. didn't
16. May   20. aren't   22. have not, haven't

Answers for items 23–25 may vary.

23. I don't put any cream in my quiche.
24. She says there isn't anything wrong with using milk.
25. We don't have any cream, anyway.

26. went   28. written   30. known
27. drove   29. knew

UNIT III

1–4.
                April 2, 1999
Dear Danny,
   I'm planning to visit my uncle in Los Angeles this summer. Will you be in town during the first two weeks in August? Let's get together!
           Your friend,
           James

5–8. <Student's address should be at upper left.>

    Mr. James Kwan
    12121 Pine St.
    Beverly, MA 01915

9. James and Danny went to Santa Monica Beach last weekend.
10. "Do you ever see movie stars here in Los Angeles?" asked James.
11. "No, most of the movie stars live in Malibu or Pacific Palisades," Danny said.
12. "Once I saw Sean Penn in a coffee shop," he added.

13–14. bikes, beach   15–16. store, sandwiches

17. men   21. Danny's   25. Danny
18. dairies   22. women's   26. store
19. wolves   23. movie stars'   27. James
20. beaches   24. temperature

28. "There's something on your towel!" yelled Danny.
29. A small, nervous crab scuttled off Rick's towel.
30. That little crab's shell had red, beige, and white markings.

UNIT IV

1. Dogs, humans, years   13. Jessica and me
2. Skipper, master, sheep   14. he
3. They, us   15. her and me
4. She, him   16. Jessica and I
5. I   17. She bought it.
6. He   18. They wagged them.
7. They   19. Now she is wagging her tail at him.
8. We
9. me   20. here
10. him   21. like
11. us   22. he
12. her   23. to

24–25. Babies cry when they are hungry.
    Australian shepherds help humans herd sheep and cattle.
    Most pet dogs are loyal and friendly.
26–28.   Jenny and Max are Maude's pups. They have silky ears, cold noses, and feet that are too big

for them. Maude feeds her pups and keeps them clean. Sometimes they seem to get on her nerves, however. Then she barks at them.

29. <u>famous</u> cartoon dogs include <u>goofy</u>, <u>snoopy</u>, and <u>odie</u>.
30. <u>charlotte</u> asked, "<u>isn't</u> <u>snoopy</u> a character created by <u>charles schulz</u>?"

UNIT V

1. Mrs. Linda Elder
2. Mr. Daniel Pine
3. Dr. Frank Ortiz
4. Gov. Andrew Kirsch
5. Ms. or Miss Sophie Kamin
6–10. Answers may vary.

<student's address>
<today's date>

Manager
The Golden Paintbrush
5665 Mesquite Blvd.
San Antonio, TX 78212

Dear Manager:
    Please send me a free catalog of your art supplies. Thank you very much.
                    Sincerely,
                    <student's signature>

11. short	17. won	23. lying
12. long	18. know	24. lie
13. la-bel	19. blue	25. lay
14. yo-gurt	20. Its	26. lay
15. mod-el	21. lay	27. lie
16. tim-id	22. laid	

28. "<u>can</u> you cook any <u>asian</u> dishes?" <u>trish</u> asked.
29. "<u>yes</u>, <u>i</u> learned to cook in <u>beijing</u>, <u>china</u>," Kam Yung replied.
30. "<u>our</u> family moved to <u>los angeles</u>, <u>california</u> in <u>september</u> 1992," she continued.

UNIT VI

| 1. flew | 3. was | 5. We | 7. us |
| 2. went | 4. become | 6. me | |

8. That tarantula's fangs pump digestive fluid into a cockroach.
9. The huge spider can't eat the cockroach yet.
10. It must wait until the cockroach's body has liquefied.
11. Its table manners aren't very attractive.

12. your	17. Her	22. Those
13. you're	18. its	23. set
14. their	19. their	24. sit
15. They're	20. These	25. sitting
16. My	21. themselves	

Answers will vary for items 26–28.
29. <u>stacy</u> asked, "<u>did</u> you make that drawing when you were in <u>south america</u>?"
30. <u>dr. stanley</u> replied, "<u>yes</u>, the spider I drew is named after a giant called <u>goliath</u>."

UNIT VII

1. branch	9. receive	15. rapid
2. melon	re-ceive´	16. rigid
3. title	10. B, C, D	17. bored
4. trampoline	11. The skull	18. filthy
5. tricycle	(or) the	19. selfish
6. umbrella	head	20. grate
7. could	12. *peak*	21. eight
could	13. six feet	22. Would
8. hundred	14. enemy	
hun´dred		

23. The <u>thick</u> pizza cooked ⬚slowly⬚.
24. <u>Hungry</u> guests ⬚impatiently⬚ waited for dinner.
25. were   26. himself   27. Weren't
28. <u>kelsie</u> graduated from the <u>academy</u> of <u>fine cuisine</u> in <u>new york city</u>.
29. <u>our</u> friend's graduation from cooking school was on <u>june</u> 26, 1998.
30. "<u>she's</u> going to make dinner for <u>mateo</u> and me," said <u>carmina</u>.

UNIT VIII

1. Stan paints pictures and Laura takes photographs.
2. Stan and Laura are very successful.
3. Stan is happy for Laura because she won first prize in the city arts contest.
4. Laura cannot collect the prize money until she goes to City Hall.
5–7. Answers may vary.
    Stan and Laura go to art galleries. They like to look at other artists' work because it inspires them. Stan is busy this afternoon, but Laura will go anyway.

8. Doesn't   10. aren't
9. haven't   11. Wasn't

12. Stan <u>paints</u> <u>portraits</u>.
13. Sara <u>bought</u> some <u>paintbrushes</u>.
14. Ann <u>makes</u> beautiful <u>weavings</u>.
15. Ophelia <u>has sold</u> a large <u>painting</u>.
16. That <u>painting is</u> (colorful.) predicate adjective
17. <u>Stan is</u> the (artist.) predicate noun
18. The <u>brushstrokes are</u> (dramatic.) predicate adjective

19. should	22. might not	25. Isn't
have	have	26. went
20. must have	23. heard	27. Doesn't
21. has	24. saw	

28. "<u>have</u> you ever seen <u>georgia</u> O'Keeffe's famous flower paintings?" asked <u>amy</u>.
29. "<u>her</u> work was first displayed in <u>new york city</u>, and she became one of <u>america's</u> best-known artists," said <u>richard</u>.
30. "<u>she</u> lived in many states, including <u>wisconsin</u>, <u>new york</u>, <u>south carolina</u>, <u>texas</u>, and <u>new mexico</u>," he continued.

Individual Record-Keeping Form   Student's Name _____

DIAGNOSTIC AND ACHIEVEMENT TESTS

	DIAGNOSTIC (Perfect Score: 30)	ACHIEVEMENT (Perfect Score: 30)	OBSERVATIONS
Unit I			
Unit II			
Unit III			
Unit IV			
Unit V			
Unit VI			
Unit VII			
Unit VIII			

Overall Assessment: _____

_____

_____

ORAL LANGUAGE OBSERVATION CHECKLIST

Listening   (Observe student's ability to: follow oral directions; understand passages read aloud; respond to questions; retain information presented orally.)

Date   *Task*   *Observation*

_____   _____   _____

_____   _____   _____

_____   _____   _____

_____   _____   _____

Speaking   (Observe student's ability to: use correct syntax; use standard English when appropriate; explain ideas or processes; summarize new concepts; retell stories.)

Date   *Task*   *Observation*

_____   _____   _____

_____   _____   _____

_____   _____   _____

_____   _____   _____

Overall Assessment: _____

_____

_____

Writing Rubric and Evaluation Checklists

Using the Writing Rubric. This rubric summarizes general characteristics of compositions written by students of varying levels of proficiency. Use this rubric in conjunction with the Checklists for Evaluating Composition Lessons, which appear on the next four pages, to help you evaluate students' writing.

Superior (4)

- Purpose, task, and audience (if specified) are addressed.
- Composition structure shows an understanding of the structure of the writing form.
- Ideas are well organized and elaborated upon in detail.
- Sentences are complete and correctly written.
- Capitalization and punctuation are used correctly.
- Nearly all words are spelled correctly.

Good (3)

- Purpose, task, and audience (if specified) are addressed fairly effectively.
- Composition structure shows some sense of the structure of the writing form.
- Ideas are organized, but not elaborated upon; or, writing exhibits good use of elaboration and detail, but ideas are not clearly organized.
- Most sentences are complete and correctly written.
- Most capitalization and punctuation are used correctly.
- Most words are spelled correctly.

Average (2)

- Task, purpose, and audience (if specified) are addressed to some extent.
- Organization of ideas is not apparent; little elaboration or detail is used.
- Shows some understanding of the structure of the writing form, but may have omitted key elements (such as a topic sentence or a conclusion).
- Writing may lack unity and focus; may contain nonsequiturs or sentences off the topic.
- Some fragments, run-ons, or comma splices may appear.
- Structure of some sentences is awkward or simplistic.
- A number of errors in capitalization, punctuation, and spelling occur.

Working Toward Improvement (1)

- Task, purpose, and audience (if specified) are not addressed.
- Writing lacks organization and focus: sentences may ramble; ideas seem unconnected; some sentences do not address topic.
- Writing shows little or no understanding of the structure or purpose of the writing form.
- Writing shows limited or no awareness of paragraph structure.
- Writing shows limited control of language; many sentences are incomplete or improperly structured.
- Writing contains many errors in grammar, usage, mechanics, and spelling.

Using the Evaluation Checklists. Duplicate a set of checklists for each student. Use them to assist you in evaluating each student's written work over the course of the year. To evaluate each writing lesson, check the box next to each item the student has completed correctly. Then add the checkmarks and record the score on the line. In addition to this score, give each writing assignment an overall score based on the Writing Rubric.

Checklists for Evaluating Composition Lessons

Student's Name_____

Use check marks to indicate items answered correctly and objectives fulfilled.

LESSON 10: Writing a Descriptive Paragraph

Read a Descriptive Paragraph

Item   *Correct Response*
- ❑ 1.   an old guitar
- ❑ 2.   The first sentence should be underlined.
- ❑ 3.   It is the first sentence.
- ❑ 4.   Possible response: **sight**—*wood . . . darkened into a nut-brown color;* **smell**—*old wood and polish cedar;* **sound**—*deep, rich sound; simple chords*
- ❑ 5.   The author values the guitar a lot.
- ❑ 6.   Possible responses: *favorite, old, worn, nut-brown, deep, rich, pleasant.* Accept other adjectives, as well.

Write a Descriptive Paragraph Check whether the student has
- ❑ selected an appropriate topic.
- ❑ identified details that appeal to the senses. (Review the web students completed. Some topics may only lend themselves to two or three types of sensory descriptions.)
- ❑ revised the paragraph. (Review the first draft and have the student explain how it was revised.)

Evaluating the Description Check whether the student has
- ❑ understood the purpose of a descriptive paragraph.
- ❑ begun the paragraph with a topic sentence.
- ❑ given several supporting details in the body of the paragraph.
- ❑ used colorful words and phrases that appeal to the senses.
- ❑ used complete sentences.
- ❑ used correct capitalization and punctuation.
- ❑ displayed the use of original language.
- ❑ given a sense of how he or she feels about the possession.

Perfect Score: 17 Student's Score: _____ Rating Scale **4 3 2 1** (*See* Rubric p. 61)

LESSON 21: Writing a Personal Narrative

Read a Personal Narrative

Item   *Correct Response*
- ❑ 1.   Any one of the following pronouns should be underlined: *I, me, my, mine, we, our.*
- ❑ 2.   that she had always wanted to fly in a small plane, and that she finally got the chance to try it
- ❑ 3.   In the middle she describes the ride itself and how awful it was.
- ❑ 4.   She ends it by telling what she was thinking about on the ride home.
- ❑ 5.   Possible responses: **when**—*fourteenth birthday; worst hour of my life; on the ride home;* **where**—*airfield; over there; farmland; Chicago; ride home*
- ❑ 6.   Possible responses: *when; what followed; after; then; finally*
- ❑ 7.   Any sentence that shows the writer's feelings should be underlined.

Write a Personal Narrative Check whether the student has
- ❑ selected a personal experience as a topic.
- ❑ identified key events in sequence.
- ❑ evaluated the first draft critically, and revised it.

Evaluating the Personal Narrative Check whether the student has
- ❑ used the first-person voice.
- ❑ correctly used the pronouns *I, me, my, we,* and *our.*
- ❑ included a beginning, a middle, and an end.
- ❑ made the setting (time and place) clear to the reader.
- ❑ described feelings as well as events.
- ❑ begun a new paragraph with each change of speaker, idea, time, or place.
- ❑ used complete sentences.
- ❑ used capitalization and punctuation correctly.
- ❑ spelled each word correctly.

Perfect Score: 19 Student's Score: _____ Rating Scale **4 3 2 1** (*See* Rubric p. 61)

Student's Name _____

Use check marks to indicate items answered correctly and objectives fulfilled.

LESSON 32: Writing a Problem/Solution Paragraph

Read a Problem/Solution Paragraph

Item   Correct Response

❑ 1.   He wanted to go to the World Series, but the tickets were sold out and he didn't have enough money anyway.

❑ 2.   The sentences that begin with these words should be underlined: *I faced two stumbling blocks . . . ; First, the tickets . . . ; Second, even if I could . . .*

❑ 3.   The last six sentences state the solution.

❑ 4.   The first four sentences should be circled.

❑ 5.   yes, because he really wanted to go to the World Series, and he got his wish

Write a Problem/Solution Paragraph Check whether the student has

❑ selected a problem from personal experience as a topic.

❑ identified pertinent background information.

❑ evaluated the first draft and made revisions to improve it.

Evaluating the Problem/Solution Paragraph Check whether the student has

❑ described a problem in the first part of the paragraph.

❑ described a solution in the second part of the paragraph.

❑ used the first-person voice.

❑ told how he or she felt about the solution.

❑ included pertinent information, not unimportant details.

❑ used correct paragraph form.

❑ used complete sentences.

❑ used punctuation and capitalization correctly.

Perfect Score: 16   Student's Score: _____ Rating Scale **4   3   2   1** (*See* Rubric p. 61)

LESSON 43: Writing a Persuasive Paragraph

Read a Persuasive Paragraph

Item   Correct Response

❑ 1.   The sentences beginning with these words should be underlined: *I feel that this change will be . . . ; For the reasons above . . .*

❑ 2.   toward the beginning and toward the end of the paragraph

❑ 3.   Stars should be placed by facts: *board members approved a regulation; the school board took a poll.* Accept other reasonable responses.

❑ 4.   The sentences beginning with these words should be underlined: *They found that many of the kids . . . ; I think it's terribly sad that . . .* **Emotional words:** *feel bad about; sad; embarrassed*

❑ 5.   Write to the school board and tell them how you feel.

Write a Persuasive Paragraph Check whether the student has

❑ understood that the writing process is broken down into five distinct steps.

❑ brainstormed different topic ideas, and chosen one.

❑ organized facts and emotional appeals before writing.

❑ understood the purpose of a first draft.

❑ revised the first draft. (Ask the student to show you the first draft and describe what he or she did to revise it.)

Evaluating the Persuasive Paragraph Check whether the student has

❑ stated an opinion in the first part of the paragraph.

❑ restated the opinion in the last part of the paragraph.

❑ included facts that support the opinion.

❑ included an emotional appeal and at least one emotional word.

❑ given readers a call to action at the end of the paragraph.

❑ used correct capitalization, spelling, and punctuation.

Perfect Score: 16   Student's Score: _____ Rating Scale **4   3   2   1** (*See* Rubric p. 61)

Student's Name _____

Use check marks to indicate items answered correctly and objectives fulfilled.

LESSON 54: Writing a Paragraph of Information

Read a Paragraph of Information

Item   Correct Response
- ❑ 1.   raccoons in the city
- ❑ 2.   The first sentence should be underlined.
- ❑ 3.   at the beginning
- ❑ 4.   An X should appear next to each fact (most sentences in the paragraph state facts.)
- ❑ 5.   it's active mostly at night
- ❑ 6.   **Physical Features**—*clever hands, sharp teeth and claws;* **Abilities**—*prowl streets at night; open jars and lids; eat anything they can find in a city; open pet doors*

Write a Paragraph of Information Check whether the student has
- ❑ selected a familiar animal as a topic.
- ❑ listed several physical features and abilities.
- ❑ used the organizer to plan the paragraph.
- ❑ revised the paragraph.

Evaluating the Paragraph of Information Check whether the student has
- ❑ included a topic sentence.
- ❑ given supporting details in the body of the paragraph.
- ❑ included facts about the animal's physical features and abilities.
- ❑ explained unfamiliar terms.
- ❑ used complete sentences.
- ❑ demonstrated proper use of capitalization and punctuation.
- ❑ spelled most words correctly.

Perfect Score: 16 Student's Score: _____ Rating Scale **4 3 2 1** (*See* Rubric p. 61)

LESSON 65: Writing a Paragraph About a Process

Read a Paragraph About a Process

Item   Correct Response
- ❑ 1.   The first sentence should be underlined.
- ❑ 2.   1; 6; 5; 2; 4; 3
- ❑ 3.   Possible responses: *first, before, next, then, as, once, for several days; after that*
- ❑ 4.   Possible responses: *wedging (getting the air bubbles out by pounding); kiln (special oven for heating pottery); bisque firing (first firing); glaze (special paint used to color pottery)*

Write a Paragraph About a Process Check whether the student has
- ❑ chosen a process that can be explained in a paragraph.
- ❑ found the information needed to explain the topic.
- ❑ identified special terms to explain.

Evaluating the Paragraph About a Process Check whether the student has
- ❑ named the process in the first sentence.
- ❑ explained the steps of the process in order.
- ❑ used sequence words to clarify order.
- ❑ given the meanings of special terms.
- ❑ used complete sentences.
- ❑ used correct capitalization and punctuation.
- ❑ spelled most words correctly.

Perfect Score: 14 Student's Score: _____ Rating Scale **4 3 2 1** (*See* Rubric p. 61)

Student's Name _____

Use check marks to indicate items answered correctly and objectives fulfilled.

LESSON 76: Writing a Paragraph of Explanation

Read a Paragraph of Explanation

Item   *Correct Response*
- ❑ 1.   how to succeed in high school
- ❑ 2.   The first sentence should be underlined.
- ❑ 3.   schoolwork, social life, and other activities
- ❑ 4.   incoming freshmen
- ❑ 5.   Possible responses: classes can be difficult; many students join clubs; high school is full of chances to learn and do new things
- ❑ 6.   The star should be by the last sentence.

Write a Paragraph of Explanation Check whether the student has
- ❑ identified an audience and purpose.
- ❑ used the organizer to list facts and opinions to include.
- ❑ revised the paragraph. (Review the first draft and have the student explain how it was revised.)

Evaluating the Paragraph of Explanation Check whether the student has
- ❑ included a topic sentence.
- ❑ included a concluding sentence.
- ❑ demonstrated an awareness of audience and purpose.
- ❑ used language and reasons that appeal to the audience.
- ❑ included both facts and opinions.
- ❑ used complete sentences.
- ❑ capitalized and punctuated correctly.
- ❑ spelled most words correctly.

Perfect Score: 17 Student's Score: _____ Rating Scale **4 3 2 1** (*See* Rubric p. 61)

LESSON 87: Writing a Story

Read a Story

Item   *Correct Response*
- ❑ 1.   A box should be drawn around the names *Matt* and *Aaron*.
- ❑ 2.   Possible responses: **where**—*hot Georgia sun; downtown; Central Station;* **when**—*August; four days after* (Students might also identify details that show the story takes place in the present, such as mountain bikes, sporting goods store, and pawn shop.)
- ❑ 3.   Sentences that define the problem appear in the second paragraph. Accept reasonable responses.
- ❑ 4.   Sentences that show the resolution appear in the last paragraph.
- ❑ 5.   An X should appear by each bit of dialogue.

Write a Story Check whether the student has
- ❑ understood that the writing process is broken down into five distinct steps.
- ❑ used the prewriting step to plan the story.
- ❑ understood the purpose of a first draft.
- ❑ revised the first draft to improve it.

Evaluating the Story Check whether the student has
- ❑ included a beginning, a middle, and an end.
- ❑ used the third-person point of view.
- ❑ included details that reveal the setting (time and place).
- ❑ understood the structure of a story.
- ❑ included characters.
- ❑ used dialogue and punctuated it correctly.
- ❑ begun a new paragraph with each change of idea, time, place, or speaker.
- ❑ spelled most words correctly.

Perfect Score: 17 Student's Score: _____ Rating Scale **4 3 2 1** (*See* Rubric p. 61)

Answer Keys for Student Lesson Pages

Lesson 1

PART I

1. yes	4. yes	7. yes	10. no
2. yes	5. no	8. no	
3. no	6. no	9. yes	

PART II

Answers will vary.

Lesson 2

PART I

1. S (.)	4. Q (?)	7. Q (?)	10. E (!)
2. Q (?)	5. S (.)	8. Q (?)	11. S (.)
3. E (!)	6. E (!)	9. S (.)	12. Q (?)

PART II

Answers will vary.

Lesson 3

PART I

1. o'Donnell, commack, new york
2. united states, ireland
3. rosie
4. rosie
5. barbra streisand, bette midler
6. o'Donnell
7. long island
8. dickinson college, boston university
9. tom hanks, meg ryan
10. o'Donnell, rockefeller center
11. fiftieth street, sixth avenue, manhattan
12. mike douglas, merv griffin
13. anne rice, pat conroy
14. o'Donnell, parker jaren, chelsea belle

PART II

Answers will vary.

Lesson 4

1. richmond, oregon
2. richmond, john day river
3. many, oregon, california, nevada, utah
4. the, richmond
5. mr. caleb n. thornburg, richmond
6. some, gilburgs, donnellys, walterses
7. a, oregon's
8. the, oregon, united states
9. r. n. donnelly, william walters
10. mr. donnelly, mr. walters "jeff davis," walters
11. perhaps, jefferson davis, confederate states, america
12. then, donnelly, richmond
13. richmond, virginia, confederate states, america

14. later, mr. donnelly
15. people, richmond
16. a, richmond methodist church
17. the wheeler county pioneers, richmond
18. many, richmond
19. people, richmond, prineville
20. one, richmond

Connecting Meanings: *luminous—shining; ominous—menacing; ludicrous—ridiculous.* Sentences will vary.

Lesson 5

PART I

1. Why are all those people wearing boots, bolo ties, and Stetson hats?
2. Tomorrow is the first day of the Calgary Stampede, Cheryl.
3. Men, women, and children dress in western styles during the Stampede.
4. Is the Calgary Stampede a rodeo, Jeannie?
5. Yes, it's one of the largest in North America.
6. Is the Calgary Stampede more exciting than the rodeo in Cheyenne, Wyoming?
7. I think all of them are exciting, Cheryl.
8. My cousin from Llano, Texas, hopes to become a rodeo rider.
9. I've seen her practice roping, bulldogging, and trick riding.
10. She's usually tired, dusty, and bruised afterward.
11. Cheryl, is there any reason why we shouldn't join in the square dance?
12. No, not unless your toes are tender.
13. Maybe we should grab some flapjacks, bacon, and coffee instead.

PART II

14. We're going to a rodeo in New York City, New York.
15. Mac, have you ever watched the event called saddle bronc riding?
16. A saddle, a halter, and one rein are placed on a bronco.
17. The rider tries to stay on that horse while it jumps, plunges, and bucks.

Lesson 6

PART I

1. is	6. were	11. was
2. is	7. was	12. were
3. were	8. were	13. was
4. were	9. were	14. was
5. was	10. were	15. were

PART II

16. were
17. were
18. are
19. is

Name That Job: *photographer.* Paragraphs will vary.

Lesson 7

PART I

1. Sun.
2. Wed.
3. Sat.
4. Mar.
5. July
6. Oct.
7. Mon.
8. Thurs.
9. Jan.
10. Apr.
11. Aug.
12. Nov.
13. Tues.
14. Fri.
15. Feb.
16. May
17. Sept.
18. Dec.

PART II

19. Dr. Betty
Klimkowski
1620 W. Main St.
Freeport, NY 11520

20. Mr. Arturo Ramirez
602 Buena Vista Ave.
Tucson, AZ 85700

21. Miss Linda Coelho
1121 NW 20th St.
Richmond, VA
23200

22. Judge Homer Yee
1548 12th Ave.
San Francisco, CA
94122

Lesson 8

PART I

1. Does Christine still want to be a reporter, Sally?
2. Yes, Sam, she has been hired by a television station.
3. Will I see her on the six o'clock news tonight?
4. Yes, she will be covering the mayor's speech.
5. How lucky she is to have such a great job!
6. Sam, Christine didn't get her job by being lucky.
7. She studied speech and journalism at Louisiana State University.
8. Christine has learned to speak, write, and think clearly.
9. She admires the work of Charlayne Hunter-Gault, Cokie Roberts, and Diane Sawyer.
10. Don't you think they are talented, intelligent, and well spoken?
11. Perhaps Christine will become a reporter for a national network.
12. No, Christine says that she prefers to live here.
13. New Orleans, Louisiana, is an exciting place to live.

PART II

14. Christine speaks in a strong, clear, pleasant voice.
15. Has she interviewed anyone famous?
16. Yes, Sam, she talked with our governor last week.
17. How I wish I had a job like hers!
18. Maybe you should take courses in speech, journalism, and political science.

Lesson 9

Granville T. Woods was an inventor. <u>he</u> created many important electrical devices. <u>several</u> of these have helped Americans live happier, safer lives. <u>some</u> people have compared Woods to Thomas Edison.

Woods was born in 1856 in Columbus, Ohio. <u>he</u> had to leave school when he was ten years old. <u>he</u> then worked at several factory jobs. <u>he</u> always paid close attention to how the factory machines worked.

Woods first became interested in electricity when he was sixteen. <u>at</u> that time electricity was just beginning to be used. <u>he</u> read many books about electricity. <u>later</u>, in 1881, he opened a factory that made electrical equipment.

Woods invented two important things in 1884. <u>the</u> first item was an improved furnace to produce steam heat. <u>the</u> second item was a telephone transmitter. <u>the</u> transmitter was something like the voice transmitters in today's telephones.

In later years Woods invented a system that let the engineer on a moving train talk with people in railroad stations. <u>this</u> invention made travel by train much safer. <u>he</u> also invented several electric trolley systems. <u>he</u> is the inventor of the third rail, which many rapid transit systems use today.

Word Whiz: *gizzard; buzzard; blizzard*

Lesson 11

1. Answers will vary.
2. Nikki, does Juan live in Portland, Maine?
No, Juliette, he lives near Faneuil Hall in Boston, Massachusetts.
Three great people of Boston were John Adams, Sam Adams, and Abigail Adams.
3. Answers will vary.
4. Answers will vary.

Lesson 12

1. The topic is the giant panda.
2. The paragraph describes the giant panda and its habitat and diet.
3. The topic is the work of firefighters.
4. The paragraph describes work that firefighters do besides fighting fires.
5. The topic is the threat of a flood.
6. The paragraph tells what might cause the flood to occur.

Lesson 13

Answers will vary.

Gorillas may look fierce, but they really are not. They are the largest of all apes. Adult males may weigh as much as 450 pounds, and adult females usually weigh about 200 pounds. Gorillas are intelligent and powerful, but very shy. They live together in family units and eat fruit, bark, and leaves. Unless they feel threatened, gorillas usually do not attack people or animals.

Lesson 14

PART I

1. Anita said, "<u>my</u> uncle is a miner, too."
2. "<u>he</u> doesn't mine coal, though," she continued.
3. "<u>what</u> kind of miner is your uncle?" asked Judy.
4. "<u>he</u> works in a salt mine in Texas," Anita replied.
5. Zack said, "I thought salt was found only in seawater."
6. "<u>salt</u> comes from mines, wells, the sea, and even lakes," said Anita.
7. "<u>my</u> uncle likes working in a salt mine," she continued.
8. "<u>his</u> mine is in an underground mountain of rock salt," she explained.
9. Judy said, "I think that's called a salt dome."
10. "<u>can</u> you tell me how salt is mined?" asked Zack.

PART II

11. Anita said, "The miners cut and drill deep into a wall of salt."
12. "Then they set off an explosive charge," she continued.
13. "The explosion makes the wall of salt collapse, doesn't it?" asked Judy.
14. Anita said, "Yes, and then the salt is loaded onto a moving belt."

Synonym Watch: *meddle — interfere*

Lesson 15

PART I

1. "We're going to talk about conserving energy," said Ms. Nakai.
2. Mrs. Simic said that all people should lower their thermostat settings.
3. "We already keep ours at 65 degrees during the day," said Mrs. Jones.
4. Ms. Nakai then asked her how she keeps herself warm.
5. "I usually wear a turtleneck and a sweater," Mrs. Jones answered.
6. "Our thermostat is set at 55 degrees during the night," said Miss Mah.
7. Ms. Nakai explained that she turns off the heat in her home at night.
8. "You must freeze!" exclaimed Mrs. Simic.
9. "We close off the rooms we're not using," said Mrs. Jones.
10. Mrs. Simic asked whether Mrs. Jones also closed the heat registers in those rooms.
11. "Yes, Mrs. Simic, I do," answered Mrs. Jones.

PART II

12. Mr. Pritchard said, "Everyone should do less driving."
13. Mrs. Simic said, "I bought a bicycle last week."

14. She explained, "Riding a bicycle helps conserve energy."

Lesson 16

PART I

1. taught	3. taught	5. learn
2. learned	4. taught	6. teach

PART II

7. May	10. can	13. May
8. can	11. may	14. can
9. may	12. Can	15. may

Connecting Meanings: *culinary — having to do with cooking; culminate — reach the highest point; cultivate — grow.* Sentences will vary.

Lesson 17

PART I

1. isn't	6. didn't	11. won't
2. aren't	7. hasn't	12. shouldn't
3. wasn't	8. haven't	13. wouldn't
4. weren't	9. hadn't	14. couldn't
5. doesn't	10. can't	

PART II

15. is not, isn't	21. have not, haven't
16. does not, doesn't	22. was not, wasn't
17. is not, isn't	23. were not, weren't
18. was not, wasn't	24. did not, didn't
19. are not, aren't	25. would not, wouldn't
20. do not, don't	

Lesson 18

Sentences may vary.

1. We can't drive this old car anymore.
2. We don't have enough money to buy a better one.
3. Maybe we can afford a used car that doesn't have any extras.
4. There are no bargains on some car lots.
5. Nobody has ever made a bad deal at Quality Motors.
6. They have nothing but good cars at fair prices.
7. A few dents don't bother me at all.
8. We don't want a car without a radio, though.
9. Let's not waste any more time talking.
10. I hope our old car doesn't lose any more oil on the way to the lot.

Lesson 19

PART I

1. seen	6. took	11. ridden
2. seen	7. written	12. drove
3. saw	8. driven	13. went
4. known	9. rode	
5. gone	10. seen	

14. That horse has broken the track record.
15. The trainer did her work well. (or) The trainer has done her work well.
16. Now she has gone to the stables. (correct)
17. A photographer has gone with her. (or) A photographer went with her.
18. She has already taken some pictures of the horse. (or) She already took some pictures of the horse.
19. The owner rode away in a big limo. (or) The owner has ridden away in a big limo.
20. He said, "I knew I had a winner!" (correct)

Lesson 20

PART I

1. thrown	7. came	13. thrown
2. came	8. came	14. saw
3. written	9. threw	15. written
4. known	10. come	16. went
5. did	11. came	
6. went	12. did	

PART II

Answers will vary.

Lesson 22

1. Answers will vary.
2. "<u>who</u> watched <u>michael</u> <u>jordan</u> on TV this <u>saturday</u>?" asked <u>gail</u>.
   <u>gina</u> said that she had watched him in the playoffs.
   "<u>gail</u>, do you think <u>jordan</u> is the best athlete in the <u>united</u> <u>states</u>?" asked <u>laverne</u>.
   "<u>well</u>, he is the greatest player in the history of the <u>national</u> <u>basketball</u> <u>association</u>," she said.
   <u>suddenly</u> <u>gina</u> shouted, "<u>i</u> have a great idea!"
   <u>she</u> said that they should create their own pro basketball Web site.
3. Answers will vary.

Lesson 23

PART I

1. Heading
2. Greeting (or Salutation)
3. Body
4. Complimentary close
5. Signature

PART II

Answers will vary.

Lesson 24

PART I

Mr. Lars Johnson
7109 N. Kelleher Ave., Apt. 103
Houston, TX 77001
Return addresses will vary.

Miss Joan Goldman
1442 S. Winston Ave.
Boulder, CO 80301
Return addresses will vary.

Lesson 25

Answers will vary.

Lesson 26

1. I read an interesting article in a fashion magazine.
2. It was about a Chinese American fashion designer named Anna Sui.
3. Anna Sui grew up in Detroit, Michigan.
4. She always wanted to be a fashion designer.
5. Ms. Sui attended Parsons School of Design in New York.
6. For years she struggled to make a living sewing her designs in her apartment.
7. Isn't Ms. Sui known for mixing different styles?
8. Her big break came when she won the Perry Ellis Award.
9. "Don't you think this outfit would look great on me?" I asked my friend.
10. "I wish I could be a fashion designer!" she exclaimed.
11. "Anna Sui has worked hard to become a success at the occupation she loves," I replied.

Lesson 27

PART I

1. <u>Cooperstown</u>, <u>foot</u>, <u>Otsego</u> <u>Lake</u>
2. <u>times</u>, <u>Mohicans</u>, <u>lake</u>, *Ote Saga*
3. <u>Cooperstown</u>, <u>William</u> <u>Cooper</u>
4. <u>son</u>, <u>James</u> <u>Fenimore</u> <u>Cooper</u>, <u>novelist</u>
5. <u>people</u>, <u>book</u>, *The Deerslayer*
6. <u>characters</u>, <u>books</u>, <u>Hawkeye</u>. <u>Uncas</u>
7. <u>Cooperstown</u>, <u>museums</u>
8. <u>Fenimore House</u>, <u>museum</u>. <u>art</u>, <u>history</u>
9. <u>Farmers' Museum</u>, <u>collection</u>, <u>pioneers</u>
10. <u>museum</u>, <u>National Baseball Hall of Fame and Museum</u>
11. <u>Baseball</u>, <u>Cooperstown</u>, <u>century</u>
12. <u>people</u>, <u>Abner Doubleday</u>, <u>game</u>
13. <u>Doubleday</u>, <u>shape</u>, <u>field</u>
14. <u>Players</u>, <u>Hall of Fame</u>, <u>sportswriters</u>
15. <u>The National Baseball Museum</u>, <u>exhibits</u>
16. <u>photographs</u>, <u>champions</u>, <u>year</u>
17. <u>photograph</u>, <u>Cincinnati Red Stockings</u>

PART II

Answers will vary.

Lesson 28

1. pioneers	14. foxes	27. dairies
2. rockets	15. women	28. cities
3. orchards	16. men	29. countries
4. products	17. feet	30. flies
5. canals	18. teeth	31. berries
6. prairies	19. journeys	32. pennies
7. rivers	20. joys	33. knives
8. mountains	21. donkeys	34. halves
9. beaches	22. valleys	35. shelves
10. wishes	23. monkeys	36. wolves
11. classes	24. factories	37. leaves
12. speeches	25. bakeries	
13. bunches	26. colonies	

Lesson 29

PART I

The second part of each answer will vary.

1. cat's	6. pilot's
2. engines'	7. mechanic's
3. flower's	8. men's
4. passengers'	9. doctors'
5. children's	10. managers'

PART II

11. The wind's speed
12. the people's achievements
13. a friend's book
14. the twins' picture

PART III

15. Mrs. Weaver's	17. Dr. James's
16. Gil's	18. Marlins'

Lesson 30

PART I

The following words should be underlined:

1. birds	7. Food, gifts
2. spot	8. Buzzards
3. festival	9. candies
4. day	10. Parents, children
5. It	11. T-shirts, buttons
6. Townspeople, visitors	12. Cars, trucks, buses
	13. people

PART II

Answers will vary.
Connecting Meanings: *reserve—set aside; preserve—protect; deserve—be worthy of.* Sentences will vary.

Lesson 31

PART I

1. Nina brought out drop cloths, brushes, scrapers, and metal ladders.

2. "Allie, do you know how to paint around window glass?" asked Nina.
3. "No, Nina, I don't," replied Allie.
4. Then she said, "I will scrape away the cracked paint."
5. Marcos remarked that Allie's idea was a good one.

PART II

Answers will vary.

Lesson 33

1. Answers will vary.
2. Answers will vary.
3.

streams	stream's	streams'
sashes	sash's	sashes'
women	woman's	women's
turkeys	turkey's	turkeys'
bodies	body's	bodies'
lives	life's	lives'

4. Answers will vary.

Lesson 34

PART I

The following words should be underlined:
1. people, golf, weekends
2. people, patience, golf
3. golfers
4. players, game, age
5. Tiger Woods, person
6. boy, Tiger, father
7. Tiger, Cypress, town, California
8. man, tournaments
9. Nancy Lopez, player
10. years, Nancy, players
11. golfers, Ms. Lopez

PART II

The following words should be underlined:

12. They	16. He	20. She
13. They, it	17. he, him	21. she
14. They	18. He	22. They, her
15. They, it	19. He, them	

Lesson 35

PART I

1. I	3. We	5. They
2. She, I	4. She	6. He, I

PART II

7. she	9. she	11. I
8. she	10. they	

PART III

Answers will vary.

Lesson 36

PART I

1. me
2. her, me
3. her, me
4. me
5. us
6. her
7. her, me
8. her, me
9. us
10. them

PART II

Answers will vary.

PART III

Answers will vary.
Odd Word Out: *statue; Possible categories: poetry; sculpture*

Lesson 37

PART I

1. us
2. We
3. us
4. we
5. we
6. us

PART II

7. He, she, it
8. She, him, her
9. she, he
10. She, he
11. He, her, them
12. she, them

Lesson 38

PART I

1. I
2. I
3. me
4. I
5. me
6. I
7. me
8. me
9. me
10. I
11. me

PART II

12. Sue and I
13. She and I
14. Fred and me
15. Sue and me
16. She and I
17. her and me
18. She and I
19. her and me
20. Sue and I

Lesson 39

First paragraph:
The following sentences should be marked out:

I'd never buy a car without a radio.
It's not easy to pass your first driver's test.
A new paint job can make an old car pleasant to drive again.

Second paragraph:
The following sentences should be marked out:

Baseball is often called the national pastime.
St. Louis is the largest city in Missouri.
The 1996 New York Jets football team had a poor record, too.
Word Whiz: *convert; invert; divert; revert*

Lesson 40

Answers may vary.

   Jill decided to have a party at the skating rink. She invited Ray, Annette, and Robyn to the party. Ray and Annette accepted immediately. They really love to skate. Robyn did not respond to the invitation right away. Finally, though, she called Jill to accept the invitation. Jill assured Robyn that she would have fun. Afterward, Robyn was glad she decided to go to the party. She had a great time! Jill taught her how to skate backwards, and Ray and Annette performed some amazing jumps. He landed a double toe loop, and she landed a double axel! Robyn later told them that they were the best skaters she had ever seen.

Lesson 41

PART I

The following words should be crossed out:

1. he, like
2. went, and
3. at
4. he
5. go, and
6. went, and
7. to
8. on
9. here
10. he, like
11. it, like, thing
12. go, and, of
13. went, and, like
14. of, up
15. he, there
16. went, and
17. like, there

PART II

18. Aladdin hurried home and showed his mother the lamp.
19. When she tried to clean it by rubbing it, another genie appeared.
20. That genie helped Aladdin become very rich.

Lesson 42

PART I

1. yesterday i finished reading one of bonnie's books about colorado history.
2. it's called the life of an ordinary woman.
3. it was written by anne ellis.
4. the book is about life in the old-time colorado mining towns.
5. anne ellis lived for a long time in the san luis valley.
6. this valley is bounded by the sangre de cristo mountains on the east.
7. farms in this high, fertile, rocky valley fed the gold miners.
8. a steep road led up from the valley to bonanza, sedgwick, exchequerville, and kerber city.
9. villa grove was the main town in the san luis valley.
10. its store had a sign offering fresh eggs, rubber boots, and corsets.

11. Bonnie asked, "Did you enjoy Ms. Ellis's sense of humor?"
12. I replied, "Yes, I really did."
13. In the book, Ms. Ellis said, "I'd gone up the gulch at six and come down at sixteen."
14. "Ms. Ellis called one road a rare specimen of engineering skill," Bonnie said.
15. "She said that a vehicle could get over it without upsetting," Bonnie continued.
16. "What a gritty person Ms. Ellis must have been!" I said.

Lesson 44

1. Answers will vary.
2. He and she enjoyed it very much.
   I saw them at the ice cream shop after it.
   He talked to her about it.
3. The following words should be crossed out:
   he; at; here; like; it, got; like; he, like, of; go, and

Lesson 45

PART I

1. Miss (Ms.) Gladys T. Faatui
2. Mrs. (Ms.) Mary Anne Abdallah
3. Dr. Helen Magid
4. Gov. T. Y. Wong
5. Judge Karla Christensen
6. Dr. Andrew O'Connell
7. Prof. (Dr.) Lee S. Sieminski
8. Sgt. Connie Branca
9. Sen. Rodney M. Jones
10. Miss (Mrs., Ms.) Sue L. Enomoto

PART II

Answers will vary.
Odd Word Out: *banker.* Possible categories: *elected officials*; *people who work in businesses*

Lesson 46

Greetings may vary.

1. Miss Joan Donaldson
   1442 Third Street
   Gilroy, CA 95020

   Dear Miss Donaldson:

2. Primo Auto Painting
   1880 Lincoln Avenue
   Cleveland, OH 44101

   Dear Manager:

3. Mr. A. B. Guliford
   Rest-a-Sured Motel
   1723 Ebenezer Street
   Cedar Rapids, IA 52401

   Dear Mr. Guliford:

Lesson 47

21 Althoff Avenue
Lansing, MI 48900
June 8, 1999

Electric Automobile Magazine
5500 Market Street
Tyler, TX 75701

Dear Editor:

I sent for the free copy of your magazine. Your ad said that I did not have to pay unless I wanted to order the magazine. Now you have sent me a bill for a year's subscription. I will not pay this bill because I did not order a subscription.

Sincerely yours,
Pat Sims

Word Whiz: *describe; prescribe; subscribe*

Lesson 48

Headings, greetings, closings, and signatures will vary.

Inside address:
Magic Miniboats
Box A-775
Trenton, NJ 08609
(or)
The Ridge Ranger Co.
645 Gale Blvd.
Roanoke, VA 24001

Lesson 49

PART I

1. pa-per
2. ta-ble
3. va-cant
4. ce-dar
5. lo-cate
6. se-cret
7. pi-rate
8. po-ny
9. do-nate
10. bu-gle
11. wag-on
12. cam-el
13. med-al
14. pen-cil
15. sol-id
16. fig-ure
17. pun-ish
18. min-ute
19. sen-tence
20. com-ic

PART II

21. ri-fle
22. riv-er
23. la-bor
24. mu-sic
25. bun-dle
26. si-lent
27. rob-in
28. lem-on
29. bo-nus
30. fe-ver
31. cab-in
32. un-der

Lesson 50

PART I

1. Who's
2. whose
3. hear
4. Here, Blue
5. whose
6. it's
7. sun
8. know
9. blew, through
10. won
11. great, too
12. to, by
13. son
14. You're, two
15. see, hair
16. buy, new
17. to, one
18. one, your, too
19. No, know
20. Its
21. meet

PART II

Answers will vary.

Lesson 51

PART I

1. lying
2. lying
3. lying
4. lying
5. lain
6. lain
7. lie
8. lie
9. lies
10. lying
11. lay

PART II

12. lay
13. laid
14. laid
15. lay
16. laying
17. lay
18. laid

Lesson 52

PART I

1. lying
2. laid
3. lay
4. lying
5. laid
6. laid
7. lying
8. lay
9. laid
10. lain
11. laid
12. lie
13. laid
14. lie

PART II

Answers will vary.

Lesson 53

PART I

1. "val, can you tell us when the First Continental Congress met?" asked the instructor.
2. "i think it met on september 5, 1774," said val.
3. elena said, "patrick henry was at that meeting in philadelphia, pennsylvania."
4. "what happened to crispus attucks in boston, mass-achusetts?" asked the instructor.
5. "he was an african american who was shot by british soldiers," said louis.
6. elena said, "paul revere warned americans that the british were coming."
7. the instructor said, "h. w. longfellow wrote a famous poem about paul revere's ride."
8. "on june 17, 1775, a famous battle was fought in massachusetts," said val.
9. "oh, that was the battle of bunker hill!" exclaimed elena.
10. louis said, "abigail adams made many important reports about british troops and ships."

PART II

11. "Louis, do you know who led the American attack on Fort Ticonderoga?" asked Val.
12. "Yes, it was Ethan Allen," replied Luis.
13. Louis added that he had read a book called America's Ethan Allen.

14. Elena explained that Mercy Warren was another who helped to win independence for America.

Lesson 55

1. Answers will vary.
2. Answers will vary.
3. Answers will vary.
4. ti-tle   mem-ber
   grum-ble ro-bot
5. Answers will vary.

Lesson 56

PART I

1. was
2. learned
3. came
4. went
5. came
6. taught
7. began
8. begun
9. became
10. began
11. wasn't
12. are
13. ran
14. weren't
15. have
16. lay
17. flew
18. Can

PART II

Answers will vary.

Lesson 57

PART I

1. us
2. I
3. us
4. We
5. me
6. she, us
7. She, us
8. us
9. Alison and me
10. They
11. her
12. Alison and I
13. I
14. We
15. me
16. her
17. Alison and I

PART II

Answers will vary.

Find the Goof: I have not *heard* a word you have said.

Lesson 58

PART I

Answers for objects possessed will vary.

1. nation's
2. Ms. Azarin's
3. Charles's
4. children's
5. friends'
6. Lucy's
7. guitar's
8. Minnesota Vikings'

PART II

9. I'd
10. you'll
11. they've
12. I'm
13. it's
14. I'll
15. we're
16. I've

PART III

17. They aren't afraid of falling.
    They're not afraid of falling.
18. It's not easy to jump over a broomstick.
    It isn't easy to jump over a broomstick.
19. I hope you aren't planning to go down that hill.
    I hope you're not planning to go down that hill.

Lesson 59

PART I

1. You're 2. Your 3. you're 4. your

PART II

5. There	9. there	12. their
6. their	10. There	13. They're, their
7. They're	11. there	14. there
8. their		

PART III

Answers will vary.

Lesson 60

PART I

1. My	5. her	9. its
2. his	6. their	10. their
3. your	7. my	11. her
4. our	8. Their	12. Their

PART II

13. its	16. It's	19. theirs
14. There's	17. There's	
15. it's, there's	18. It's	

Lesson 61

PART I

1. those	5. These	9. these
2. these	6. these	10. Those
3. these	7. those	11. those
4. those	8. these	

PART II

12. herself	15. himself
13. themselves	16. themselves
14. herself	

Antonym Watch: *deny—affirm*

Lesson 62

PART I

1. sat	6. set	11. set
2. set	7. sit	12. set
3. sit	8. sitting	13. sit
4. set	9. set	14. sets
5. set	10. setting	15. sits

PART II

Answers will vary.

Lesson 63

Answers will vary.

Lesson 64

PART I

1. cassie said, "i need a book to read on friday, lucinda."
2. "have you read a book called *black elk speaks* yet?" asked lucinda.
3. cassie said, "no, i don't think i have."
4. "it was written by john g. neihardt," said lucinda.
5. "it was based on his visit with black elk," she continued.
6. "was black elk a member of one of the dakota tribes?" asked cassie.
7. lucinda replied, "yes, he was one of the oglala sioux."
8. "the dakota once rode the plains from canada to the black hills," cassie remarked.
9. "black elk was a wise person and a spiritual leader," said lucinda.
10. "he was second cousin to crazy horse," she continued.

PART II

11. "Where did Mr. Neihardt meet with Black Elk?" asked Cassie.
12. Lucinda said, "They met on the Pine Ridge Reservation in South Dakota."
13. "I'm going to read about Black Elk," said Cassie.
14. Then she asked, "Did you know that my father's grandmother was a member of a Dakota tribe?"

Lesson 66

When you're riding a bicycle, you must always watch the road ahead of you. When we friends drove to work yesterday, we saw an accident in front of Mrs. Wilson's store. A cyclist wasn't paying attention to the cars parked along the street. A driver opened a car door, and the cyclist ran right into it. He crumpled to the pavement, and his head struck the cement. Fortunately, he was wearing a safety helmet.

The driver of the car threw a jacket across the cyclist and sat beside him until the traffic officer came. When the ambulance arrived, the medics laid the cyclist on a stretcher and took him to the hospital. Someone said that the cyclist's leg was broken. The officer took the names of us people who had seen the accident.

Lesson 67

PART I

1. city	4. gulf	7. radar
2. dock	5. history	8. television
3. forest	6. ocean	9. zoology

PART II

10. altitude	13. bay	16. camera
11. ancient	14. boundary	17. clothes
12. artist	15. burden	18. curtain

PART III

19. bench
20. beside
21. better
22. cello
23. center
24. certain
25. dollar
26. donate
27. doughnut

PART IV

28. champion
29. chance
30. chart
31. drift
32. drill
33. drive
34. emperor
35. employ
36. empty

Lesson 68

PART I

The following words should be underlined:

1. similar
2. finally
3. peaceable
4. making
5. height
6. length
7. privilege
8. receive
9. coming
10. believe

PART II

11. at´las
12. ex-press´
13. ze´bra
14. re-move´
15. ter´ror
16. de-light´
17. thun´der
18. ar-range´
19. a-part´ment
20. hol´i-day
21. de-vel´op
22. re-mem´ber
23. won´der-ful
24. hap´pi-ness
25. el´e-gant
26. com-mu´ni-ty
27. bi-ol´o-gy
28. im-pos´si-ble

PART II

Answers may vary.

29. ran
30. ruf
31. grim´e
32. chek
33. groth
34. kem´ist
35. fiz´iks
36. chel´o

Lesson 69

1. amphibian
2. five
3. Spanish
4. Indiana
5. four
6. lean
7. receive
8. 39.37
9. three
10. after the *w*
11. minor
12. all
13. football
14. dessert
15. the third
16. Arabic
17. five
18. a tropical fruit (or) the kind of tree that the soursop fruit grows on
19. 5,280
20. bi
21. not
22. sheep

Lesson 70

PART I

1. search
2. inside
3. obtain
4. labor
5. unusual
6. aid
7. melody
8. raise
9. impolite
10. weep

PART II

Answers will vary.

11. Will we be able to save the old building?
12. The residents of our town love that building.
13. We have raised enough money to restore it.
14. A skilled contractor is directing the project.
15. I hope this elegant building will stand forever.

Lesson 71

PART I

Answers may vary.

1. never
2. smile
3. front
4. fall
5. leave
6. beginning
7. brave
8. weak
9. calm
10. early
11. sadness
12. reject
13. few
14. busy
15. light
16. after
17. tight
18. empty

PART II

Answers may vary.

19. neat, messy
20. old, new
21. over, under
22. buy, sell

Name That Job: *farmer*. Paragraphs will vary.

Lesson 72

PART I

1. read, great
2. know, Greece
3. Some, not
4. There
5. know, their
6. It's
7. sun, by
8. sum, one
9. know
10. your, days, one, you're, right
11. two
12. heard, tales, there
13. There
14. Would, to
15. see, red, some
16. too
17. No, week, too, there
18. ate
19. buy
20. by

PART II

Answers will vary.

Lesson 73

PART I

The following words should be underlined:

1. wise, talented, powerful
2. first, small, African
3. famous
4. coastal
5. early, pleasant, carefree
6. bright, young, skillful, agricultural
7. many, unusual, wild, west

The following words should be underlined:

8. quickly
9. gradually
10. extremely
11. Later
12. consistently
13. often
14. beautifully, forcefully
15. continually
16. Today, wisely

Answers will vary.

Lesson 74

1. was
2. saw
3. is
4. came, took
5. saw
6. into
7. ran
8. learned
9. Those, were
10. weren't, in
11. went, into
12. himself
13. Doesn't
14. We
15. done
16. laid
17. set
18. in, seen
19. any
20. are
21. is
22. themselves

Answers will vary.

Lesson 75

1. on tuesday, february 18, 1998, my friend hannah was snickering, gurgling, and howling.
2. "hannah, what's so funny?" i asked.
3. "haven't you looked through this book yet?" she asked.
4. "no, i've never seen it before," i answered.
5. i noticed that the book's title was *cat*.
6. it was a book of cartoons by b. kliban.
7. i said, "hannah, i'd like to borrow this book."
8. "oh, i'm sorry," she said.
9. "i've already promised it to ted, rachel, bill, molly, john, heidi, igor, and connie," she said.
10. then she told me that she would show me her favorite drawing.
11. it showed the difference between a cat and a meat loaf.

12. I told Hannah that I didn't see the humor in the drawing.
13. But on February 20, 1998, I looked at Pureheart, our lazy Burmese cat.
14. I saw that Pureheart did look a lot like a meat loaf.

Odd Word Out: *sonnet* should be circled; astronomy, kinds of poems

Lesson 77

1. mag´net   pro-pose´
   light´ning   cred´it
   ma´jor   de-mand´
2. call   slant
   chat   sleep
   chop   slope
   cloud   spare
   coal   spell
   core   spring
   creek   stand
   crest   stick
   crib   sting
3. S   S
   S   A
   A   S
4. Answers will vary.

Lesson 78

1. Realtors sell houses and condominiums.
2. Realtors must know neighborhoods and property values.
3. Buyers and sellers are often anxious.
4. Realtors are always looking for listings and buyers.
5. Sometimes realtors work two months and make nothing, and sometimes they work two hours and make $10,000.
6. Buyers have different needs and tastes.
7. A realtor learns what people like and shows homes that fit their taste.
8. Ms. Moseley has a sunny personality and years of experience selling real estate.
9. She showed us a four-bedroom home and said it was a good buy.
10. That house was too large and too expensive for us.

Lesson 79

Answers will vary.

1. When I arrived at the camp, a guide named Angela met me.
2. She showed me to my tent, where I stowed my gear.
3. The cook made a great meal over the campfire, but I didn't eat much.
4. When I get nervous, I lose my appetite.
5. After we finished dinner, Angela gave a talk on the history of the Grand Canyon.
6. Before John Wesley Powell began an exploration of the Colorado River canyons in 1869, he had four boats made.
7. Powell and his group traveled hundreds of miles on the river between steep canyon walls, and they became the first non-native people to explore the Grand Canyon.
8. Although Powell's wooden boats were sturdy, they were not easy to maneuver.

9. Today most river runners use rubber rafts because they are easy to maneuver.
10. You don't know real fear until you've faced the 25-foot wave of Crystal Rapids.

Lesson 80
Answers will vary.

Imogen Cunningham was a great American photographer. She began taking photographs in 1901, and she continued for more than seventy-five years.

Some of Cunningham's photographs are realistic, and others show things that are strange and fantastic. She took pictures of people, interesting objects, and plants. She is especially famous for her portraits of Hollywood movie stars of the 1930s.

Imogen Cunningham's photographs have been displayed in museums throughout the world. Her photos also appear in many photography books. She truly was an artist with a camera.

Lesson 81

PART I
1. Don't
2. Aren't, isn't
3. haven't
4. doesn't, haven't
5. hasn't
6. doesn't
7. isn't
8. haven't
9. wasn't
10. Aren't
11. don't
12. doesn't
13. isn't
14. haven't
15. haven't
16. haven't
17. Don't, aren't
18. Doesn't
19. Wasn't
20. wasn't
21. isn't

PART II
Answers will vary.
Word Whiz: *translation; transfusion; transportation*

Lesson 82

PART I
1. crashed, motorcycle
2. has ridden, wheelchair
3. caused, problems
4. wanted, mobility
5. built, wheelchair
6. could climb, stairs
7. designs, wheelchairs
8. has designed, airplanes
9. present, challenge
10. fly, airplanes
11. travels, paths
12. admire, designs
13. builds, chairs
14. arranged, workshop
15. hold, equipment
16. loves, work
17. patents, designs
18. can use, them
19. founded, Whirlwind Wheelchair Network
20. helps, riders
21. build, chairs
22. provide, independence
23. won, Chrysler Award

PART II
Answers will vary.

Lesson 83
1. Traffic is heavy; predicate adjective
2. Sidewalks are crowded; predicate adjective
3. city can seem cold; predicate adjective
4. Chinatown is neighborhood; predicate noun
5. Portsmouth Square is park; predicate noun
6. It is island; predicate noun
7. park is popular; predicate adjective
8. Warren Suen is native; predicate noun
9. Chinatown has been home; predicate noun
10. he was member; predicate noun
11. he became gardener; predicate noun
12. job is difficult; predicate adjective
13. Care is test; predicate noun
14. Clean-up, maintenance are time-consuming; predicate adjective
15. work can seem endless; predicate adjective
16. Warren Suen was gardener; predicate noun
17. He was caretaker; predicate noun
18. He was friend; predicate noun
19. residents felt lonely; predicate adjective
20. Warren Suen is hero; predicate noun

Lesson 84

PART I
1. has
2. should have
3. must have
4. has
5. must have, heard
6. might not have
7. any
8. must have
9. grew
10. drew
11. Haven't, any
12. wrote
13. grew
14. heard
15. has
16. must have, heard

PART II
17. I should have known that the city was founded by Lord Baltimore.
18. The city has many elegant mansions.
19. You couldn't have dragged me away from the aquarium with a tow truck.
Connecting Meanings: *principal—person with authority; principle—important rule; principality—land ruled by a prince.* Sentences will vary.

Lesson 85

PART I

1. There
2. doesn't
3. Have, eaten
4. are
5. are
6. Those, there
7. went
8. their
9. ours
10. are
11. us, eaten
12. are
13. seen
14. They're
15. are
16. is
17. Doesn't
18. eaten
19. are, its
20. Doesn't
21. their

PART II:

Answers will vary.

Lesson 86

PART I

1. "gail, i don't even know what a hydrofoil is," said lani.
2. "you'll soon find out," said gail.
3. the two friends stood by the harbor of the city of charlotte amalie.
4. beyond the harbor lay the caribbean sea.
5. they were leaving st. thomas to visit gail's relatives, the sánchezes, in san juan, puerto rico.
6. "here comes the hydrofoil!" exclaimed gail.
7. "i'm not sure i want to ride in that," said lani quietly.
8. "oh, come on!" said gail.
9. they stood in line, walked forward, and finally stepped aboard.
10. "its name is the canaria," remarked gail.
11. soon the canaria was cruising over the ocean surface.
12. "we're traveling almost forty-five miles an hour!" a passenger said to lani.

PART II

13. "Yes, and we're being propelled by two high-speed water jets," added Gail.
14. She then explained that the hydrofoil has struts which reach down into the sea.
15. Afterwards Lani said that the trip had been smooth, quick, and pleasant.
16. Gail said, "Yes, hydrofoils run smoothly even in six-foot waves."
17. "Gail, I'm really enjoying my Caribbean vacation," said Lani.

Lesson 88

1. Answers may vary.
   Jodie Foster is a fine actress and a noted director and producer.
   She has been acting since she was two years old and has appeared in many movies.
   She attended Yale University and graduated with highest honors in 1985.
2. Answers may vary.
   Her desk is clean, but my desk is cleaner.
   Because I've worked the hardest, I deserve the award.

3. com-mand-ing   roll-ing
   toss-ing   swim-ming
   can-ning   suf-fer-ing
4. Answers will vary.

Lesson 89

PART I

1. no
2. no
3. yes (.)
4. no
5. no
6. yes (.)
7. yes (?)
8. no
9. yes (.)
10. yes (!)
11. yes (.)
12. no

PART II

Answers will vary.

Lesson 90

Answers will vary.

Inside address:
All-Truck Parts Company
1357 N. Industrial St.
Chicago, IL 60607
(or)
All-Seasons Fashions
495 Flatbush Ave.
Brooklyn, NY 11238
Odd Word Out: *locomotive.* Possible categories: *ships;
railroad cars*

Lesson 91

PART I

1. firefighters
2. children
3. selves
4. chimneys
5. dogs
6. matches
7. men
8. mice
9. feet
10. calves
11. rallies
12. oxen
13. wharves
14. attorneys

PART II

15. Mrs. Hawkins's
16. Lois's
17. Richard's
18. class's
19. women's
20. Americans'
21. classes'
22. horse's
23. soldiers'
24. Ross's
25. entry's
26. kitten's
27. people's
28. Kelly's

PART III

29. we've
30. you've
31. she's
32. can't
33. doesn't
34. I'll
35. aren't
36. they're
37. won't
38. shouldn't
39. that's
40. you're
41. couldn't
42. don't

Lesson 92

PART I

1. "What's that machine in your back yard?" asked Al.
2. "That's an oil well," said Dolores.
3. "No, really, what is it?" asked Al.
4. Dolores told him she was telling the truth.
5. "I thought oil wells were huge," said Al.
6. Dolores explained that small oil wells are quite common.
7. "In fact, more than three quarters of the oil wells in the United States are small," she said.
8. "Is there a special name for a small oil well?" asked Al.
9. Dolores said, "A well that produces less than ten barrels a day is called a stripper."
10. Then she said that more than 400,000 wells in the U.S. are strippers.
11. Al asked, "Does your family make much money from your well's production?"
12. Dolores told Al that they did.
13. Al said that he wouldn't mind having an oil well in his back yard.

PART II

14. Then Al said, "Maybe I should drill there."
15. Dolores said, "Drilling there probably isn't a good idea."
16. She said, "Drilling for oil is very expensive."
17. Al asked, "When was your well drilled?"
18. She said, "My grandparents drilled it many years ago."

Lesson 93

PART I

1. know
2. heard, there
3. you're, see
4. shone
5. It's, blue
6. to, one

PART II

Synonyms will vary. Sentences will vary.

7. cut
8. huge
9. grouchy
10. stay
11. pick
12. let
13. smiling
14. present

PART III

Antonyms will vary. Sentences will vary.

15. fresh
16. outside
17. old
18. fast
19. enemy
20. seldom
21. open
22. lose

Lesson 94

PART I

1. is
2. taken
3. are
4. gone
5. have
6. weren't
7. began
8. come
9. are
10. seen
11. wasn't
12. could have
13. done

PART II

Answers will vary.
Word Whiz: *beneficial; superficial; artificial*

Lesson 95

PART I

1. us
2. she
3. me
4. He, I
5. I
6. him and me
7. She
8. she
9. They
10. us
11. them
12. them
13. us
14. himself
15. he
16. him
17. they
18. they
19. Medhi and I

PART II

Answers will vary.

Lesson 96

1. advise — ad-vise
2. balance — bal-ance
3. before — be-fore
4. beginning — be-gin-ning
5. describe — de-scribe
6. elbow — el-bow
7. excellent — ex-cel-lent
8. express — ex-press
9. finally — fi-nal-ly
10. hurrying — hur-ry-ing
11. justice — jus-tice
12. legally — le-gal-ly
13. missing — miss-ing
14. misspell — mis-spell
15. mistake — mis-take
16. occurring — oc-cur-ring
17. planning — plan-ning
18. shopping — shop-ping
19. toadstool — toad-stool
20. unwilling — un-will-ing
21. welcoming — wel-com-ing

Lesson 97

PART I

1. "i'm tired of watching the same old programs on TV," said jolene loudly.
2. "well, why don't you listen to the radio with me tonight?" asked leon.
3. "you mean just sit around and listen to rock?" asked jolene disgustedly.
4. "no, i'm talking about listening to old radio shows," said leon.
5. he explained that one station was playing nothing but shows from the old days.
6. she asked if he meant programs like "the green hornet."
7. "yes, that's right," leon answered.
8. "old radio shows are funnier, scarier, and more interesting than TV shows," he continued.
9. "why do you think so?" asked jolene.
10. "you can use your imagination to picture things you hear," leon said.
11. jolene said that she herself had a pretty wild imagination.

PART II

12. "We're in for some thrills on Wednesday, January 6, 2000," said Leon.
13. Jolene asked what show would be on that night.
14. Leon said that the show called "Richard Diamond, Private Detective" would be on.
15. "Weren't Dick Powell, Ed Begley, and Virginia Gregg in that?" she asked.
16. "Jolene, you know more about old-time radio than I do!" Leon said.

Lesson 98

1. no; no; yes.; yes.; no
2. "Wasn't Bret Harte born in Albany, New York, on August 25, 1839?" asked Josh.
   "Yes, this early American author liked to write about gamblers, adventurers, and miners," said Sue. Then Sue said that "The Luck of Roaring Camp" was her favorite short story.
   José said that many of Harte's story titles include the names of mining camps in California.
3. sit
   teach, lie
   Don't
4. Synonyms and antonyms will vary.

below	under	above
modern	new	ancient
victory	win	defeat

5. children, chimneys, scarves, feet, latches, berries, women, moose, flashes, shelves
6. soldier's, man's, doctors', Evelyn's, Patriots', monkey's
7. you're, we've, it's, aren't, I'll, they're, can't, won't
8. shown, too or two, four or fore, wait, main, tail, whale, your
9. I, he, us, him and me, her

INDEX OF TOPICS FEATURED IN LEVEL II
(Numbers listed are page numbers.)